# Mozambique's Experience in Building a National Extension System

# Mozambique's Experience in Building a National Extension System

Helder Gemo

Carl K. Eicher

Solomon Teclemariam

Michigan State University Press • *East Lansing*

⊛ The paper used in this publication meets the minimum requirements of
ANSI/NISO Z39.48-1992 (R 1997) (Permanence of Paper).

Michigan State University Press
East Lansing, Michigan 48823-5245
Printed and bound in the United States of America.

10  09  08  07  06  05      1  2  3  4  5  6  7  8  9  10

LIBRARY OF CONGRESS CATALOGING-IN-PUBLICATION DATA
Gemo, Helder.
Mozambique's experience in building a national extension system /
Helder Gemo, Carl K. Eicher, and Solomon Teclemariam.
p. cm.
Includes bibliographical references.
ISBN 0-87013-763-8 (alk. paper)
1. Agricultural extension work—Mozambique. I. Eicher, Carl K.
II. Teclemariam, Solomon. III. Title.
S544.5.M85G46 2005
630'.71'5—dc22
2005013003

Michigan State University Press is a member of the Green Press Initiative and is
committed to developing and encouraging ecologically responsible publishing
practices. For more information about the Green Press Initiative and the use of
recycled paper in book publishing, please visit *www.greenpressinitiative.org*

Cover and book design by Sharp Des!gns, Lansing, MI

Visit Michigan State University Press on the World Wide Web at *www.msupress.msu.edu*

# Contents

# Tables and Figures

## Tables

## Figures

# Foreword

They who are satisfied with their work have reason to be dissatisfied with their own satisfaction.

*—Multatuli*

Reflecting on the experiences made over the past seventeen years in building a national extension system for Mozambique is an indication that the National Directorate of Rural Extension is determined not to rest on its laurels of past achievements—of which this publication bears evidence—but to critically assess the progress made, take stock of the weaknesses and threats with the purpose of adjusting and further developing and improving its service delivery.

After all, it is the regular and critical assessment and evaluation of progress or past performance and the effective use of the information to improve future delivery that can contribute most towards the improvement of current and future extension. This publication bears evidence of the above motives and intentions and for this the Ministry of Agriculture should be congratulated.

As a country with one of the youngest extension services, Mozambique has the opportunity of learning from other countries' mistakes. However, associated with this is the risk of blindly following the example of other countries and this could mean blindly following the blind. A large number of countries, particularly in the developing world, have fallen prey to this. Were they overwhelmed by the experienced and more developed donor countries or did this happen because of a general lack of insight and understanding of the situation-specificity of extension delivery and its impact?

The success of an extension system is largely a function of the dynamic interaction of a multitude of factors forming part of the total situation, including the physical, social, cultural, socio-economic and organizational environments and the way these are perceived. The implication of this is that a system, approach or even method found to have been successful in one country or situation, will not necessarily be successful in another, while the opposite can also be true. While this applies generally, the implications are particularly relevant to the African situation. African countries will have to design and craft their own extension systems that are effective, sustainable and appropriate to the African and local situation. Mozambique is courageously showing and leading the way, and should be applauded.

PROF. DR. GUSTAV DÜVEL

*University of Pretoria, Department of Agricultural Economics,*

*Extension and Rural Development (South Africa)*

# Preface

Mozambique was a latecomer to independence in 1975 and in institutionalizing a public extension system in 1987. But because of the on going Civil War; public extension did not become operational until peace was achieved in 1992. Today, Mozambique has over 3 million small-scale farms (the family sector) and three extension providers: public, NGOs, and private. Since there are limited resources to expand public extension, research, and other critical agricultural services, some hard choices must be made on the size of the public extension system and the role of NGOs and private sector in delivering extension. There are also some difficult operational issues to resolve such as how to accelerate the decentralization of extension, how to improve the connectivity between research, extension and local and regional faculties of agriculture and how to determine whether poor farmers can buy their way out of poverty by paying for some of the cost of extension. Unfortunately there are few agricultural extension success stories in Africa that Mozambique can emulate. Many public agricultural extension systems are under stress in Africa. Most extension models that have been imported from other continents are not delivering the expected results. Without question, there is a crisis in extension in Africa, especially in the post conflict counties trying to strengthen the capacity of the Ministry of Agriculture.

To address these issues, the Ministry of Agriculture of Mozambique has embarked on a major reform of its basic agricultural service institutions, including extension. Since capacity building is a pragmatic process that unfolds slowly and almost invisibly over time, it is necessary to document the performance of competing extension models in terms of their ability to develop a national extension system that is pluralistic, effective and financially sustainable. An additional factor is the need to share the results of ongoing extension experiments with extension managers, policymakers and members of the donor community.

Currently, there are six basic extension models in Africa. All have been imported from other continents. The first is the public extension model that was inherited from colonial powers (in some but not all of the colonies) and then dramatically increased in size following independence in the sixties and seventies. Today, Kenya is an extreme example of a country with roughly 8,000 public extension workers, many of them are constrained by a lack of basic operating funds. The second model is the commodity extension model that was pioneered among smallholders producing cotton in Mali and other Francophone countries some fifty years ago. The third is the Training and Visit (T&V) model that was launched in Turkey in the early seventies and then spread to India and throughout Africa under World Bank sponsorship in the late seventies and the eighties. However, the T&V model has proven to be financially unsustainable. The fourth extension model is the NGO model (international and local) that spread rapidly in the nineties as many NGOs shifted gears and moved from providers of food and humanitarian assistance to become agents of development. The fifth model is the private sector model that is spreading in industrial countries such as the Netherlands and New Zealand and more recently in middle income countries such as Chile. Under the private model, the farmer is expected to pay some of the cost of extension with the hope that public outlays on extension could be reduced. The sixth and most recent model is the Farmer Field School (FFS) model that has garnered publicity in rice mono cropping farms in the Philippines and Indonesia. The model has been in operation for a few years in East Africa and more recently in Mozambique. The FFS model should be carefully studied in Mozambique to answer two questions: do the field schools increase the knowledge of farmers in the short and long run and does increased knowledge of farmers lead to higher crop yields and increased agricultural productivity?

This book chronicles the evolution of extension in Mozambique over the past seventeen years from 1987 to 2004 and reports that there is a growing recognition that crafting institutional reforms is a pragmatic, exploratory and social learning process that unfolds over years and decades. With this vision of the need for learning by doing and learning from the global experience, Mozambique is now carrying out a three-year pilot study of privatization (outsourcing) of extension delivery in the Murrupula district in Nampula province and a similar three-year study in Nicoadala district in Zambezia province. The results of this comparison of public and private delivery of extension will be published and made available to other countries in Africa and to donors.

The authors are grateful to the organizations and colleagues that have directly or indirectly contributed to the publication of this book. Many thanks for support from the Ministry of Agriculture, the Family Sector Livestock Development Program (FSLDP) of the International Fund for Agricultural Development (IFAD), PROAGRI, SG2000, and the W.K. Kellogg Foundation. Many thanks also to Peter Wagner, Custodio Mucavele, and Jose Jeje for their valuable comments and suggestions and to Fifi Hussein for her superb word processing skills.

# Abbreviations

| | |
|---|---|
| AGRITEX | Department of Agricultural and Technical Extension Services (Zimbabwe) |
| ARC | Agricultural Research Council (South Africa) |
| ASSP | Agricultural Sector Support Program |
| BMZ | German Ministry for Development Cooperation |
| CFFM | Common Flow of Funds Mechanism |
| CGIAR | Consultative Group on International Agricultural Research |
| CLUSA | Cooperative League of the USA |
| CTIA | Technical Council for Agricultural Research |
| DANIDA | Danish International Development Agency |
| DAP | Policy Analysis Department, Directorate of Economics |
| DDA | District Directorate of Agriculture |

| | |
|---|---|
| DDADR | District Directorate of Agriculture and Rural Development |
| DE | Directorate of Economics |
| DFID | Department for International Development (United Kingdom) |
| DINA | National Directorate of Agriculture |
| DINAP | National Directorate of Livestock |
| DNDR | National Directorate for Rural Development |
| DNER | National Directorate of Rural Extension |
| DNFFB | National Directorate of Forestry and Wildlife |
| DPADR | Provincial Directorate for Agriculture and Rural Development |
| DPAP | Provincial Directorate of Agriculture and Fisheries |
| DRandSS | Department of Research and Specialists Services (Zimbabwe) |
| ELC | Extension Learning Centre |
| EU | European Union |
| FAO | Food and Agriculture Organization of the United Nations |
| FARA | Forum for Agricultural Research in Africa |
| FFS | Farmer Field Schools |
| GOM | Government of Mozambique |
| GTZ | German Bilateral Agency for Development Co-operation |
| IFAD | International Fund for Agricultural Development |
| IIAM | Institute of Agrarian Research in Mozambique |
| INIA | National Institute for Agricultural Research |
| INIVE | National Institute for Veterinary Research |
| IPA | Animal Production Institute |
| JVC | Joint Venture Company |

| | |
|---|---|
| MADER | Ministry of Agriculture and Rural Development |
| MAP | Ministry of Agriculture and Fisheries |
| M&E | Monitoring and Evaluation |
| MINAG | Ministry of Agriculture |
| MPF | Ministry of Planning and Finance |
| NEPAD | New Partnership for Africa's Development |
| NGO | Non Governmental Organization |
| PROAGRI | National Agricultural Development Program |
| REPETE | Periodic Technology Review Meeting |
| SG 2000 | Sasakawa Global 2000 |
| SIDA | Swedish International Development Agency |
| SISNE | National Extension System |
| SPAAR | Special Program for African Agricultural Research |
| SPER | Provincial Extension Service |
| SUE | Unified Extension System |
| T&V | Training and Visit Extension Model |
| UEM | Eduardo Mondlane University |
| UNDP | United Nations Development Program |
| USAID | United States Agency for International Development |
| WVI | World Vision International |

# CHAPTER 1

# Introduction

A major lesson is that an agricultural extension or advisory service takes a long time to be built . . . . If a country is unwilling to invest in this time-demanding, learning, and evolutionary process, it is unlikely that it can eventually put in place an efficient and effective agricultural advisory service for small-scale farmers.

*—Berdegue and Marchant (2002)*

"Getting agriculture moving" is the acid test for the New Partnership for Africa's Development (NEPAD) because agriculture and rural nonfarm activities employ around 70 percent of the labor force in Africa; food insecurity is chronic and Africa is the poorest part of the global economy. To address these issues, NEPAD (2002) highlights the need to increase agricultural productivity, reduce climatic risk through irrigation and increase support for agricultural services, especially extension and research. However, one of the biggest challenges facing Ministries of Agriculture and Finance in Africa is how to address the institutional puzzles surrounding the near collapse of the core research and extension institutions that provide services to small-scale family farms. Unfortunately, neither donors nor academic specialists have "credible" answers on how to resolve these institutional puzzles. Today, instead of importing institutional models, a growing number of African nations are pursuing a pragmatic process of crafting a system of agricultural service institutions compatible with their culture, ideology, agrarian structure and development strategy. (Rukuni 1996; Rukuni, Blackie, and Eicher 1998).

Unlike many Anglophone and Francophone African countries that inherited large extension systems at independence, Mozambique was a latecomer in gaining independence (1975) and institutionalizing a public extension system through the establishment of the National Directorate for Rural Development (DNDR) in 1987. However, because of the then ongoing civil war, public extension did not become operational until 1992. This explains why Mozambique's public extension system is one of the youngest in the world (Gemo 2000; Gemo and Rivera 2002).

Presently, there are 1,838 extensionists employed by three major extension providers in Mozambique: public, NGOs (international and local), and private companies (especially cotton, tobacco, and cashew). The public extension service—National Directorate of Rural Extension (DNER)—has a total of 770 agents, supervisors, technical and central staff (table 1) located in 10 provinces and 66 of the 128 districts in the country. Currently there are 840 extensionists employed by national and international NGOs and 228 extension agents employed by private farms (DNER, M&A, October 2004). The basic question for policymakers is how to build a Mozambican national extension system that is pluralistic and fiscally sustainable in an environment where donors are financing the bulk of the budget of the Ministry of Agriculture (MINAG),[1] and there is a prevailing donor atmosphere of downsizing and privatizing public extension.

Mozambique has one of the newest and leanest public extension services in Africa and herein lies some of its hidden advantages. Instead of being bogged down with 8,000 extension workers like Kenya, or saddled with Zimbabwe's recently merged and troubled research and extension system,[2] DNER is a relatively lean organization with 770 public extension workers and central staff. DNER has the freedom and resources to carry out pilot studies of outsourcing and experiment with the FAO Farmer Field School (FFS) approach[3] and other participatory farmer-to-farmer extension models.

**Table 1.** Public (DNER) Extension Staffing by Province and Headquarters, 2005

| PROVINCE | EXTENSIONISTS | SUPERVISORS | | PROVINCIAL LEVEL | TOTAL |
|---|---|---|---|---|---|
| | | TEAM | NETWORK | SPER | |
| Maputo | 37 | 4 | 0 | 5 | 46 |
| Gaza | 57 | 8 | 3 | 5 | 73 |
| Inhambane | 43 | 6 | 3 | 8 | 60 |
| Sofala | 77 | 2 | 11 | 10 | 100 |
| Manica | 62 | 6 | 6 | 9 | 83 |
| Tete | 40 | 6 | 0 | 7 | 53 |
| Zambézia | 48 | 6 | 0 | 9 | 63 |
| Nampula | 88 | 10 | 11 | 10 | 119 |
| Niassa | 46 | 6 | 1 | 7 | 60 |
| C. Delgado | 78 | 9 | 3 | 4 | 94 |
| *Subtotal* | 576 | 63 | 38 | 74 | 751 |
| *DNER Central Staff* | | | | | 19* |
| *Total DNER* | | | | | 770 |

Source: DNER, February 2005.
*Includes four resident consultants.

In principal, the geographical coverage of the extension system includes the entire ten provinces in the country. The coverage is supplied in part by the public extension service in selected areas, NGOs,[4] and large private farms and companies. Radio and mass media are used to reach farmers throughout the country. The Provincial Rural Extension Services (SPERs) operate in all ten provinces, but with varying degrees of coverage. Public sector extension agents are deployed according to a number of criteria such as agricultural potential, thus explaining why there is a high concentration of public extension agents in the high potential areas in the northern and central part of Mozambique.

The 1997 Extension Master Plan reported that public extension agents would be concentrated in 52 of 128 districts from 1998 to 2003, but there were DNER agents in 66 districts in year the 2004. In districts without DNER agents, DNER provides guidance to Provincial Extension Services on how to promote extension activities and implement mass media programs for maximum coverage (DNER 1997).

## Background

Mozambique reclaimed its independence in 1975 and, after a few years, it embarked on a program of central planning and the introduction of parastatals and state and cooperative farms that were primarily focused on increasing cashew nut, cotton, and food crop production. However, because of the poor performance of state-led agriculture, the government changed policy direction in the mid-1980s, and set about "freeing agriculture from the state." This new policy promoted large private farms and joint venture companies (JVCs) and private small-scale farms (the family sector). This dramatic policy shift opened the door for an institutional innovation—public extension. In 1987 the government launched a public extension service to assist small-scale farms increase food production and promote rural development. Private extension started in the early 1990s through the involvement of private and JVCs in agricultural production.

The emergence of public and private extension was a result of policy reforms of the mid-1980s that shifted priorities from parastatal production (e.g. state farms) to small-scale agricultural producers and large private farms. After peace was declared in 1992, the non-governmental organizations (NGOs) provided emergency and rehabilitation assistance and played an important role in helping farmers return to their villages and resume farming. In the mid-1990s, the NGOs shifted their attention from providers of humanitarian assistance to development and became active in implementing numerous development projects in agriculture, health, education, rural roads, etc.

In early 2005 there were 1,838 extensionists employed by three types of extension providers in Mozambique.[5] DNER in the Ministry of Agriculture is operating in 66 of the 128 districts in the country. Private extension is composed of large private farms with their own extension staff who help smallholders mainly producing cotton and tobacco on contract with the private farms. NGOs, local and international, are active in providing extension services to smallholders in parts of about 119 districts (there is overlapping with public extension in at least 40 districts).

Agriculture is the main socioeconomic activity of the people of Mozambique, and it directly or indirectly employs around two thirds of

the population (Kanji et al. 2002). In 2003, the agricultural sector has contributed an average of 25 percent of the annual GDP. Agriculture also
plays an important role in rural employment generation as well as con-
tributing to household and national food security and reducing rural
poverty. Currently, about 70 percent of the population below the absolute
poverty live in rural areas.

Mozambican agriculture is dominated by 3.3 million smallholders
(family sector) averaging 1.1 ha in size and employing about 63 percent
of the men and a high percentage of the women in the country. The smallholders contribute more than 80 percent of the annual value of agricultural production. The common denominator of small-scale producers is
low productivity, limited ability of households to generate savings and
chronic family food insecurity. These characteristics dominate small-scale
agriculture which is geographically dispersed as well as culturally, technically and economically heterogeneous. Given this overview, the challenge is one of figuring out how to develop a national extension service
capable of mobilizing the latent productive capacity of 3.3 million smallholders averaging 1.1 hectares in size.

## Why This Book?

Since Mozambique became independent in 1975 it seems logical to pose
the question: what is the justification for this book on agricultural extension that covers the seventeen-year period from 1987 to 2004? There are
several answers to this question:

❶ Because of the upheaval surrounding Mozambique's civil war in the
1980s and early 1990s, the government did not formally establish a
national public extension system until 1987, and it only became operational in 1992. Since a number of other African countries are also
currently in the post-emergency stage of development (e.g. Sierra
Leone, Liberia, the Congo, and Angola), it follows that the development of an operational and financially sustainable public extension
system is a major challenge for new governments to address. This is

an especially burning issue because extension has historically been a core activity in ministries of agriculture in Africa. However, the structural adjustment programs of the 1980s recommended downsizing and privatizing both research and extension. Therefore, one may legitimately pose the question: If extension is no longer a core activity in Africa's ministries of agriculture, what is the mission of the ministry now that many national agricultural research organizations have been spun off into independent statutory corporations and donors are also pushing hard to privatize input markets and national grain storage operations? Since Mozambique is addressing some of these issues through a learning-by-doing mode, it follows that DNER's valuable experience in developing a national extension system should be synthesized and made available to other countries in Africa and to donors and the academic community at large.

❷ The second reason why this book has been prepared is that donor funding for extension projects has been sharply curtailed in Africa in the 1990s, along with general donor cut backs in support for agriculture and an almost corresponding increase in donor outlays on rural education, health, and food emergencies (Kane and Eicher 2004). What can be done to encourage donors to reconsider and invest in improving extension in Africa?

❸ The third reason is that the seventeen-year time period covered by this book represents a sufficiently long period of time for a new institution to have a system in place and staffed with professionals and delivering services. The World Bank, for example, conducted a global review of its research and extension projects in the mid-1980s and concluded that "Experience with the T&V technique of extension, as with others, suggest that at least ten to fifteen years are needed to get the system firmly in place and to develop a professional field-based system (World Bank 1985, viii). The experience of setting up a new privately funded development institution in the United States some fifty years ago sheds light on the current donor practice of pressing for an evaluation of new projects after two or three years. In 1951 John D. Rockefeller III invited thirty-one scientists to a two-day meeting in Williamsburg,

Massachusetts, to table a proposal to use his private fortune to establish a new organization to study world population problems. The thirty-one scientists attending the meeting endorsed his recommendation and the Population Council was set up with a global office in New York City. Mr. Rockefeller oversaw the selection of the president and board of directors of the Council and reported that he did not want a formal evaluation of the program of work until fifteen years—a period long enough to evaluate performance and identify needed changes in leadership and program direction (Population Council 1978). Today the Council is thriving and enjoys a hard-earned reputation as the world's leading population center.

❹ The 2004 ending date for this book marks the completion of the fifth and final year of the first phase of Mozambique's public agricultural sector investment program (PROAGRI) and the fifth year of the implementation of the first Extension Master Plan.

❺ Since the Ministry of Agriculture is focusing on spurring institutional innovations, it follows that the results of Mozambique's extension innovations should be published to stimulate debate and an exchange of ideas with extension managers, practitioners, and members of the academic community.

❻ The final justification for this book is to contribute new knowledge that can be used by teachers of extension and rural development courses in schools, faculties, and universities of agriculture in Africa and throughout the world, including industrial countries. We hope this study of Mozambique's experience will be supplemented with other country studies of agricultural extension and nation building in Africa, particularly in post-conflict environments.

## Objectives of Study

The general objective of this study is to analyze the evolution of agricultural extension by three types of providers (public, private, and NGOs) over the seventeen-year period from the inception of public extension in 1987 until 2004. The specific objectives are to:

- Describe the context and rationale for establishing public, private, and non-governmental extension providers.
- Discuss the three main types of providers in terms of their philosophy, objectives, target groups, methodologies, and access to resources.
- Describe the role of the government, external financiers, and relevant services (agricultural research, input and output markets) in relation to the three extension providers.
- Synthesize the extension experience from the past seventeen years and draw lessons for the future of extension in Mozambique.

This study is divided into eight chapters covering the three principal phases of the history of agricultural extension in Mozambique. The first phase from 1987 to 1992 covers the establishment of public and private extension during the on-going Civil War. The second phase from 1993 to 1998 covers the strengthening of public and private extension and the emergence and rapid expansion of non-governmental (NGO) extension. The third phase from 1999 to 2004 analyzes the changing roles of public, private, and NGO extension within a pluralistic environment of service provision. The study draws lessons from seventeen years of experience and lays out an agenda of challenges that should be debated and addressed during the implementation of the second Extension Master Plan over the 2005–9 period (DNER 2004).

The principal sources of data for this study have been compiled from an exhaustive review of quantitative and qualitative information from the public extension service, interviews with nearly all of the private firms providing extension services, and more than half of the international NGOs involved in extension. Informal and formal interviews were conducted with technical managers of the three extension providers. Coordinators, program directors, and senior managers of NGOs, private firms, and public sector were also interviewed. Since public and NGO extension depends nearly exclusively on external finance, it was also necessary to review the documentation of multilateral and bilateral development agencies such as the World Bank, FAO, UNDP, IFAD, USAID, DFID, EU, DANIDA, and GTZ. Informal interviews were also carried out with agricultural and rural development officers, especially with donor representatives supporting agricultural extension.

District and local authorities were also asked about the role and performance of extension. Interviews were conducted with approximately 30 percent of the district administrators and 50 percent of district directors of agriculture and rural development in areas where public, private, and NGOs operate. Informal interviews were also conducted with leaders of producer organizations in five provinces and with the unions of producer organizations such as the National Union of Farmers (UNAC).

Numerous field visits were made to observe the three types of extension providers in action. Data collection was carried out from 1999 to 2003 in the central and northern regions of the country where about 70 percent of agricultural extension work is carried out.

Most of the documented information was obtained from the three main extension service providers (private enterprises, NGOs, and public sector) and from the records of various donors involved in financing agricultural extension. Some information from the early years of public extension was not available. But sufficient information was collected to document the establishment, changing roles, and challenges facing the three extension service providers. Since the focus of this study is drawing lessons from experience, we shall now summarize rural institution building in Africa and extract lessons for policymakers and extension providers in Mozambique.

## NOTES

1. The Ministry of Agriculture and Rural Development (MADER) was renamed the Ministry of Agriculture (MINAG) in early 2005.
2. Zimbabwe recently added 2,000 extension workers (to its 4,000 base) to assist newly settled farmers. Zimbabwe has around 6,000 extensionists in the Department of Agricultural Research and Extension (AREX) and around 865 livestock extentionists in its Livestock Production and Development Department (Tawonezvi 2003).
3. For an empirical study of the FFS approach in Peru see (Godtland et al. 2004).
4. Forty-two NGOs, mostly international, were delivering extension services when the first Extension Master Plan was prepared in 1997 (DNER 1997).
5. The 1,838 extentionists in Mozambique in early 2005 were employed as follows: DNER 770; NGOs 840, and private 228.

# Building Rural Institutions in Africa: Painful Lessons

**W**ithout question, rural institutions are in considerable disarray in Africa. Since Mozambique's experience with public extension is relatively brief (1987–2004), it has much to learn from Africa's painful lessons in institution building starting with the first wave of independence in the early sixties. Mozambique also has much to learn from the global experience of the past forty years. For example, after three to four decades of accretionary (step-by-step) institution building, many countries such as Malaysia, Thailand, and Brazil have developed a world-class agricultural science base and technology transfer system and have become powerhouses in global agricultural trade. Can Mozambique build a strong system of agricultural service organizations in twenty to thirty years, a feat that has taken forty years in Brazil? Much depends on the ability of Mozambique to mobilize political, scientific, farmer, and donor support and stay the course for a period of decades (Eicher 1999).

The following examples illustrate the crisis in rural institutions in Africa:

- Kenya is one of many African countries where public agricultural extension is nearly immobilized. Kenya currently has around 8,000 extension workers as a result of the recent absorption of extension workers in crops, livestock, fisheries, and cooperatives into the portfolio of the Ministry of Agriculture. But Kenya's extension service has nearly collapsed due to the lack of financial sustainability of the T&V (Training and Visit) extension model.[1] Although there is government agreement on downsizing Kenya's extension service, there are not adequate funds and political support to carry this out. By contrast, Mozambique's public agricultural extension service is seventeen years old and it has 770 public extension workers. Nevertheless, even though there are approximately 8,000 public extension workers in Kenya and 770 in Mozambique, the managers of both of these national extension services must answer a common question: how can public investments in extension be justified when so many public extension systems in Africa are ineffective and financially unsustainable (Nielson and Bazeley 2000; Nielson 2002).

- Human capital degradation arising from HIV/AIDS and the steady migration of public extension officers and researchers to NGOs and the private sector are undercutting the buildup of a stable cadre of public agricultural extension and research officers in many countries in Africa. A few years ago, twenty Zambian agricultural researchers were sent overseas for postgraduate study. Although nineteen of the twenty returned home, only four of the nineteen are currently employed by the public research service in Zambia. The other fifteen left for higher salaries with NGOs and the private sector. In Mozambique, from 1999 to 2003, a number of M.Sc. and B.Sc. graduates with experience left the National Institute of Agronomic Research (INIA) to join NGOs and other organizations. Although the World Bank has recommended doubling the annual expenditure on agricultural research in Africa (from US$1 to 2 billion per year), it does not address the revolving door question of how to stop the outflow of scientists to better paying jobs with NGOs and the private sector and the international brain drain (Ndulu 2004).

Human capital degradation is a severe constraint on building a national agricultural science base and efficient and sustainable delivery systems for a modern agriculture. Few African ministries of agriculture have marshaled the scientific capacity to make "informed policy decisions" on controversial topics such as agricultural biotechnology and the WTO. Moreover, even if an African government embraces biotechnology, where is the critical mass of scientists necessary to sort out biotechnology research priorities and then actually carry out the research (Byerlee and Fischer 2002)? The same type of challenge faces African countries in trying to figure out how the Ministries of Agriculture should deal with the consolidation of food retailing as witnessed by the growth of supermarkets in Southern Africa (Weatherspoon and Reardon 2003) and the intricacies of the WTO (Binswanger and Lutz 2001).

- South Africa's new agricultural strategy reports that "support services to farmers in the former homeland areas have all but collapsed" (South Africa 2001, 9). Moreover, South Africa's Agricultural Research Council (ARC) is experiencing a meltdown in its scientific base. Forty-five scientists with a Ph.D. have left the ARC in recent years. The main reason is the sharp cutback in the Parliamentary allocation to the ARC over the past four years (Agricultural Research Council 2000-1).[2] The government has also mandated that 50 percent of ARC's future budget should come from contract research, a requirement that will undermine the ability of the ARC to carry out public good research to assist smallholders.

- The Faculties and Universities of Agriculture in Africa are being challenged to reexamine their raison d'etre in an era of biotechnology, information and communications technology (ICT) and globalization. Increasingly, the following question is being posed: are African faculties and universities of agriculture becoming obsolete in an era of biotechnology which requires inputs from experts throughout the university community such as molecular biologists in faculties of science, bio-safety and legal experts in faculties of law and guidance from faculties of commerce (business administration) on how to mobilize venture capital for biotechnology projects.[3]

- Many African nations have abruptly changed institution-building strategies and, in the process, they have unwittingly wiped out decades of hard-fought gains in capacity building. Zimbabwe, for example, recently merged its public research (DR&SS) and extension service (AGRITEX) with the goal of reducing administrative costs, but after four years of implementation, the merger is mired in controversy. Also, Tanzania abruptly abolished its Ministry of Cooperatives and Ministry of Local Government in the 1970s and then reintroduced cooperatives in the 1980s. Tanzania recently transferred its national extension service from the Ministry of Agriculture to the Ministry of Local Government, but it did not set up an Extension Secretariat in Dar es Salaam to provide overall direction, monitoring and evaluation. These unilateral and ad hoc shifts in institutional arrangements have been extremely debilitating. Instead of pursuing ad hoc reforms similar to those in Zimbabwe and Tanzania, the government of Uganda has been praised because it is pursuing a measured, comprehensive and a 25-year period of restructuring its agricultural institutions, including a restructuring of extension, research and Makerere University (Crowder and Anderson 2002; Friis-Hansen and Kisauzi 2002 and Nahdy et al. 2002).

## Painful Lessons

What can Mozambique learn from these painful lessons of building rural institutions? Four lessons emerge from the Pan African and global experience that are relevant to the current institutional restructuring of MADER and DNER.

### ■ Political Leadership and Commitment for the Long Pull

The most important lesson from the Pan African and global experiences in institution building is the need for African political leadership to provide a reliable flow of domestic and donor funds to slowly and methodically build a sustainable system of interactive rural institutions over a period of decades. Farmers and farm organizations have a powerful role to play in building a national agricultural science base and a technology delivery system that is relevant to their needs. Farmers and farmer associations should channel their research needs and priorities to the Institute of Agricultural Research and their economic policy concerns to the political leadership at district, provincial, and national levels. After all, political leadership in the State House coupled with demand side pressures from farmers and clientele groups played a critical role in building a productive system of agricultural service institutions in Malaysia, Taiwan, India, Brazil, Uruguay, and Chile. Turning to Africa, one can observe that clientele pressures represent an integral part of the reforms of rural institutions that are currently underway in Uganda and Mali. Unfortunately, many donors have underestimated the time and cost of helping African nations build sustainable systems of agricultural institutions. Many donors cut their support in the 1990s to the three core institutions in the agricultural knowledge triangle: research, extension and agricultural higher education (Kane and Eicher 2004). Fortunately, the World Bank and bilateral donors have recently decided to increase their support for agricultural research and extension (World Bank 2003b). USAID has agreed to expand the number of scholarships for postgraduate training in food and agriculture both in the United States as well as strengthening faculties of agriculture in developing countries (BIFAD 2003).

### ■ Crafting a National System of Interactive Rural Institutions

Without question, there has been a failure of many imported models of rural institutions in Africa. Well-known examples include the T&V extension model, the U.S. land-grant model of higher education[4] and the Asian Green Revolution model of increasing food production. Although these failures throughout Africa are painful, they represent valuable learning experiences for Mozambique. Instead of relying only on imported institutions, Mozambique should devote primary attention to crafting a system of rural institutions that is compatible with its own history, culture, agrarian structure, political ideology and development strategy. The challenge for DNER is to build a Mozambican extension system that is pluralistic, efficient and financially sustainable.

What is meant by a system of rural institutions? Basically, it is an informal coalition of policy makers, public and private scientists and extension workers who communicate, cooperate and interact to achieve a common goal of "increasing human welfare through greater agricultural productivity" (Bonnen 1998). But raising agricultural productivity can do more than increase food production and help meet food security needs. If Mozambique focuses only on increasing food production, it would be selling agriculture short! Agriculture can make five strategic contributions to overall economic development: producing food for a growing population, earning foreign exchange, mobilizing capital, creating rural employment and serving as a market for the industrial sector. The Ministry of Agriculture should focus on pragmatically crafting a national system of rural (public and private) institutions to help agriculture fulfill its multiple roles in development at this early stage of Mozambique's economic history.

It is well known that the payoff to public and private investments in extension is critically dependent upon the performance of complementary institutions such as agricultural research, quality of rural infrastructure and access to credit and markets. Since agricultural extension is only one component of a system of rural institutions, our analysis of the evolution of extension in Mozambique since 1987 examines the degree of connectivity between extension, research, universities and farmers as well as linkages with input and product markets and producer organizations. The bottom line is that the performance of a productive system of agricultural institutions adds up to more than the sum of its individual components (Alex et al. 2002).

The use of donor-financed projects to strengthen agricultural institutions is fraught with coordination problems, high transaction costs, and donor meddling into local, provincial, and national affairs (Morss 1984). One of the painful lessons of African development is that there are high transaction costs in coordinating, reporting and evaluating an assortment of donor projects. The chief economist of the World Bank's Africa department reported that in 1999, donors sent missions to Tanzania at the rate of 1,000 per year and the government was producing 2,400 quarterly reports annually to meet the requirements of donors (World Bank 2002). In 1997, donors helped finance forty-two separate projects totaling US$43 million for Mozambique's Ministry of Agriculture (World Bank 1999). One can imagine the time and energy that it took for administrators and scientists to manage and prepare quarterly and annual reports for forty-two projects.

What is the alternative? The sectoral approach represents an alternative to the project approach in development planning and institution building. However, although numerous African countries have tried to persuade donors to co-finance comprehensive sectoral approaches to agricultural development and institution building, it has been difficult to get donors to pool their funds and stay the course and support pooled funding for a long period of time. Only a few countries such as Mozambique and Uganda have provided leadership in moving from projects to a sectoral approach to coordinating investments in the agricultural sector and pooling donor funds.

■ Time and Continuity of Domestic and Donor Funding

Time and continuity of donor funding are critical but underplayed components of building a productive and sustainable system of agricultural development institutions. It has taken many developing countries four to five decades of concentrated and dogged effort to build a strong national agricultural science base and efficient public and private delivery services. But most donors adopt a short-term time frame and support institution building for five to ten years and then move on to another country. The experience of India illustrates the payoff to political leaders who stayed the course, year after year and decade after decade.[5] Today, India has a government grain reserve of 50 million tons.

Because of Brazil's success in capacity building in agriculture, it is useful to examine how it patiently developed an impressive human capital base over a period of forty years. In 1963, the government took a high level political decision to build a human capital base for a modern agriculture. With USAID financing, four American land grant universities assisted four Brazilian universities in strengthening B.Sc. level training for a decade followed by another four years of support for postgraduate education. In 1972, the government established EMBRAPA (Brazilian National Agricultural Research Corporation) to coordinate its national research program. EMBRAPA launched a massive human capital improvement program and spent 20 percent of its total budget from 1974 to 1982 on training programs in Brazil and abroad. In fact, in the late 1970s and 1980s, EMBRAPA had an average of more than 300 researchers enrolled each year in postgraduate training programs. Today, one third of EMBRAPA scientists have a Ph.D. degree, half have M.Sc. degrees and the balance have a B.Sc. (Beintema et al. 2001). Brazil's success story should be carefully studied by MADER .The most important lesson from Brazil's experience for MADER is the fact that Brazil did not reduce its public expenditure on its core agricultural institutions some forty years ago when it began its march to build a strong human capital base and a globally competitive agricultural science base. Instead, Brazil mobilized high level political support and increased its investments in both public agricultural research and extension (Macedo 2003).

NEPAD's agricultural strategy devotes major attention to building African scientific capacity in agricultural research, extension, agribusiness, supply chain management, and international trade. The challenge for Mozambique is to develop a long-term local, regional, and global training plan that will enable it, like Brazil, to develop a formidable national agricultural science base coupled with public, nongovernmental and private technology delivery systems.

■ Sequencing of Investments

The crafting of a productive and financially sustainable system of agricultural institutions in Mozambique requires some hard decisions on the sequencing of investments in extension, research, higher education, and decisions on priorities for investments in low, medium and high potential regions.[6] Mellor (1976) reports that India concentrated on building roads and irrigation infrastructure and deployed extension agents in seventeen "high-potential" districts where the output response was assumed to be the highest. DNER, like India of the 1960s, has made a decision to concentrate its front line extension workers in high potential agricultural districts. However, there is a lack of profitable technology on the shelf for extensionists and smallholders in many of these districts.

Mozambique's agricultural research system is being reorganized. Four zonal research stations will be developed and more attention will be given to research on agroforestry and natural resource management. However, it will take a period of time before the research system acquires the capacity to deliver a steady stream of profitable technologies to extension providers and small-scale farms. In the interim, Mozambique should intensify its borrowing of technology from neighboring countries and the global research system (Eicher and Rukuni 2003). Some excellent examples of "smart" borrowing include Mozambique's recent importation of the Vitamin A–enriched sweet potatoes, cassava and improved rice varieties and small scale cassava and rice processing machines from CGIAR research centers. However, smart borrowing requires careful prioritization of applied research in order to turn imported technology into farmer adoption.

## NOTES

1. The Training and Visit (T&V) agricultural extension model was pioneered by Daniel Benor in the 1970s is a "top down" model designed to improve the management of public extension systems (Benor and Harrison 1977). It was introduced in Turkey in the seventies and later in India. The World Bank promoted the T&V model in Africa in the 1980s and by 1990 twenty-two African nations were implementing the T&V extension model. However, by the late nineties, many African nations found themselves unable to finance the model. For a critique of T&V extension performance in Kenya (see Gautam and Anderson 1999; Anderson and Feder 2004).

2. The South African Parliamentary allocation was not sufficient in 2001 to cover ARC salaries, retirement and infrastructure. The ARC was charged with fund raising from the private sector and pursuing contract research.

3. See Byerlee and Fischer (2002) for a guide to building agricultural biotechnology capacity in developing countries.

4. The U.S. Congress enacted the land-grant model of higher education in 1862 in order to serve the needs of an agrarian nation. The model allocated federal land to each state in order to provide a financial base (the land could be sold or rented) to underwrite the construction of one land-grant college (later university) per state. Each college incorporated

the triple functions of teaching, research, and extension. The model is generally regarded as a success in the United States and a failure in many developing nations because of conflicts between universities and well-established research and extension services in ministries of agriculture. Therefore, many land-grant type universities in developing countries have evolved into teaching institutions.

5.  See Lele and Goldsmith's study of India's three decades of experience (1960s–80s) in building a strong agricultural science base and an array of efficient agricultural service institutions (1989).

6.  Rice (1971) points out that most Latin American countries over invested in extension in the 1950s and 1960s because it was assumed that technology could be imported from the United States and diffused by an expanded number of extensionists. However, this turned out to be a "false start" and policymakers had to shift course and increase investments in research in Latin America in order to produce technology for local agroecologies and extension workers.

# The Introduction of Public and Private Extension in Mozambique: 1987–1992

Mozambique became independent in 1975 and, after a few years, it introduced a centralized economy, including state farms, cooperatives and agricultural parastatals. By the mid-1980s, around 130 agricultural state enterprises produced about half of the marketed production of food crops in Mozambique (Abrahmsson and Nilsson 1994). However, the failure of the central planning model and the bankruptcy of state agricultural enterprises, prompted the government to abandon cooperatives and state farms and shift to a free market ideology. This basic policy shift was an acknowledgment of the socio-economic importance and potential of the family sector and private-large scale farms. In the late 1980s, the state started to attract private investment in agriculture by forming Joint Venture Companies (JVCs) between the government and private capital, especially for the production of cash crops such as cotton and tobacco.

## The Introduction of Public Extension

In 1986, a year before the official creation of the government extension service, the Department of Rural Development (DRD) employed technicians and foremen to serve about 300,000 families in 2,227 villages. Carr (1991) reports that the rural extension services had a total of 1,100 workers: 250 were technicians with certificate and diploma level education and 850 were foremen who were recruited from the ranks of successful farmers.

Mozambique's public extension service was created in 1987 (DM No. 41/87), through the official establishment of the National Directorate of Rural Development (DNDR). The specific mandate was to provide agricultural extension services to assist in organizing farmer associations and cooperatives, and to introduce improved agronomic practices, technology and livestock practices in order to increase the production and productivity of small-scale farms and promote integrated rural development. (Boletim da Republica 1987). However, public extension was institutionalized during a period of armed conflict in the late eighties and an environment of social tension, economic, and political instability and extreme degradation of basic social services, especially in rural areas. The immediate government priorities during this period were to provide food and temporary shelter to accommodate displaced rural people throughout the country and deliver basic health services and community defense. The functioning and stability of extension in this initial phase was seriously affected by the circumstances mentioned above. In districts where extension services operated, the constant movement of people in search of secure areas made it difficult for extensionists to maintain working relationship with farmers. Even in areas of relative security, extensionists stayed in the field for only about four hours per day. Extension technicians were largely based in the capitals of districts and provinces because of the lack of security in rural communities. Under these circumstances, it was difficult to implement a normal extension program with adequate technical supervision as well as Monitoring and Evaluating (M&E) of field activities.

In 1987 the Department of Rural Development (DDR) was transformed into the National Directorate of Rural Development (DNDR) and charged with providing and coordinating extension to smallholders. During that time there were two types of extension (Caballero 1991). The first type of DNDR extension helped small-scale farms increase the production of food crops such as cereals, legumes, roots and tubers, and horticultural crops. During the initial phase, public extension limited its attention to the diffusion of simple technical messages such as line and early sowing, timely weeding and good soil preparation. The second type of extension focused on cash crops such as cashews, tea, cotton, and tobacco. Public institutions such as the State Secretariat of Cashew (1978 to 1996), of Cotton (1978 to 1994), and the Mozambican Tea Enterprise (EMOCHA 1978 to 1997) provided extension assistance for their respective crops. This type of extension was later continued by Joint Venture Companies (JVCs) to promote cash crops with emphasis on cotton through the provision of improved seed, inorganic fertilizer and pesticides on credit. The cost of inputs was deducted from farmer's accounts when they sold their cotton to the JVCs.

## Target Population, Model Adopted, and Start-Up Problems

Four factors influenced the establishment and orientation of government extension: the general objective, target population, implementation of activities and model to be adopted. The general objective of public extension has always been "to contribute to the increase of agricultural production and productivity." The family sector was defined as the priority of extension. The Training and Visit (T&V) model was adopted by the government with financial assistance from IFAD, the World Bank and the FAO. The T&V System was modified in 1993 and it is still practiced by DNER today.

The guiding principles established since the beginning of public extension stress the use of a problem-solving approach to extension. Goncalves (1992) has enumerated the guiding principles of public extension as the need:

• To be based on rural reality, that is, starting from the knowledge of concrete situations;

23

- To be in accordance with the economic, cultural and technical levels of the target population;
- To involve the target group as active participants in their development;
- To start with the problems and priorities of the target group;
- To have concrete objectives and systematic evaluation of results; and
- To be flexible and have an educational character

The guiding principles emphasize the importance of farmer participation in the formulation, implementation and evaluation of extension programs. However, the principles mentioned above are those of an institution (public extension), which aims to be a service provider to farmers. The guiding principles do not mention the role of complementary actors such as research, agricultural support service providers or input and equipment suppliers. The principles enunciated by Gonçalves did not include the participation of other extension service providers and the need to facilitate complementarities between target groups and agricultural support services.

■ Target Population

The family sector—small-scale farms—was defined as the target population for public extension for three reasons. First, the family sector was responsible for about one-third of the agricultural produce marketed from the mid-seventies to the mid-eighties. Second, the gradual collapse of state agricultural enterprises in the mid-1980s forced the government to turn to a new type of farming that did not require direct state support and responsibility. Third, large-scale private farms and the new JVCs in cotton and, in some cases tobacco, created an opportunity to provide private extension services to smallholders to produce cotton and tobacco under contract with the large farms.

The family sector is characterized by economic, religious and cultural heterogeneity and differences in values, beliefs, and habits. These factors plus and dozens of local languages and the current rate of illiteracy of 66 percent in rural areas constitute major challenges to extension.

Finally, the high level of absolute poverty in rural areas constitutes a serious constraint on the ability of farmers to purchase inputs and post-harvest technologies.

The size of smallholder farms (the family sector) ranges from 0.5 to 1.5 hectares of land and the basic agricultural inputs are seeds, simple tools and family labor. Most farmers are still using local varieties of seeds retained from their own production or acquired through informal channels. Improved seeds are used today mainly in agricultural extension areas or in zones where cash crops are being promoted and there is a demand for improved inputs. Improved seeds are also distributed free during emergency situations such as floods and droughts.

■ Model, Organization, and Functional Structure

When public extension was institutionalized in Mozambique, it adopted the Training and Visit (T&V) model. Although the model was modified by DNER in 1993, the organizational and functional structure of public extension is still following the hierarchical interaction embodied in the original T&V model. For example, network supervisors directly control extension networks at the district level. The extension network ("Rede" in Portuguese) is defined as an organic unit that ensures the implementation of agricultural extension with available human, material and financial means (Gonçalves 1992). At the provincial level, activities such as planning, M&E and communication, farmer organizations, training and field technical support were created and consolidated starting from the 1990s. Figure 1 shows that the national extension office has two departments and one support services unit: the Planning Department (Planning, Monitoring and Evaluation, Project Studies), the Technical Support Department (Field Technical Support, Communication, Training, Farmer Organizations), and the Administration and Finance Unit. The Planning, Monitoring and Evaluation Department is responsible for consolidating the preparation of the annual work plan, monitoring its implementation, and coordinating extension impact and evaluation studies. It provides technical support to the provincial M&E units in setting up and maintaining the information management system, and preparation of annual

**Figure 1.** Current Organizational Structure of the National Directorate of Rural Extension

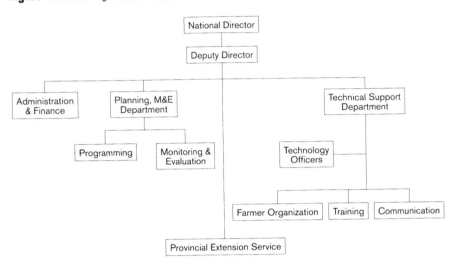

plan of activities and budget. The Technical Support Department includes technical support staff in the following areas: production technology (technology officers for different areas such as crops, natural resources, post-harvest technology and livestock), producer organizations, training, and communication.

Given the special importance of women in agriculture and the need to incorporate their perspective into extension programs, the department staff includes technical officer(s) on gender issues. DNER's national office also housed the HIV/AIDS coordinator from 2000 to 2004, and it will continue to coordinate and complement the Ministry of Agriculture's interventions at the farm household and community levels. The administration and finance unit is responsible for administering human and financial resources, following the decisions taken by those responsible at the technical level and according to the budgets established in the annual work plans.

The provincial offices provide technical, methodological and logistical support to extension networks in each district (figure 2). The provincial team includes a provincial head, a provincial technology officer, a training technician, a communications technician, a monitoring and evaluation technician, and farmer organization technician. Subject matter

**Figure 2.** Organizational Chart of Provincial Extension Service (SPER)

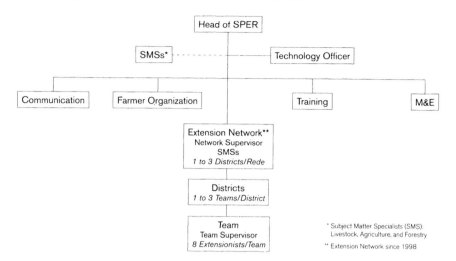

specialists from the Provincial Services within the Provincial Department of Agriculture provide technical support as part of their normal activities. All of the members of the extension team are subordinated to the Provincial Extension Head, and receive technical support and supervision from the central level. At the lower level of operation, extensionists are organized into teams within extension networks (each extension team consists of eight extensionists). Each network of eight to twenty-four extensionists provides supervision, technical support, and continuous training. The extension network unit (Rede in Portuguese) may cover parts of one, two, or three administrative districts. Team supervisors support field-level extensionists, roughly one for every eight extensionists. The extension teams are supervised by a network extension head supported by a group of up to three subject matter specialists (SMSs) in the areas of agriculture, livestock and forestry.

■ Geographical Coverage

The number of public extension networks was expanded from 28 to 46 in districts over the 1988–92 period. The functioning of the extension networks and SPERs was roughly compatible with the T&V model. DNER network supervisors usually had eight extension agents per team; a fixed agenda of visits to contact farmers and followed routine fortnightly training of extensionists. The supervisors also had a pre-established agenda of supervision. The SPER technicians in turn prepared work plans except in cases where there were financial restrictions or security problems. Likewise the central level followed a regular plan of supervision and made quarterly visits to the provinces (SPERs) and the extension networks.

■ Start-Up Problems

It was difficult to implement the T&V model from 1987 to 1992 because of security and financial constraints during the Civil War. Most of the extensionists only had a certificate or were fresh graduates with certificates. Some were experienced extensionists who had worked on state farms producing cotton, cashew and citrus. As a result, during the start up phase of public extension from 1987 to 1992, most extensionists were poorly trained to deal with the complex and diversified farming systems of small-scale farms. During the first phase of public extension from 1987 to 1992:

- DNER lacked subject matter specialists (SMSs) at network and provincial levels.
- The number of extensionists for each DNER team was variable depending on the availability of resources.
- The link between extension and research was weak.
- There was a lack of new farm practices and technologies appropriate to the circumstances of small-scale farms.

### Agronomic Practices and Appropriate Technology

The main crops in Mozambique are cereals such as maize (*Zea mays L.*), paddy rice (*Oryza sativa*), sorghum (*Sorghum vulgare*), pulses such as cow pea (*Vigna unguiculata*) butter bean (*Phaseolus vulgaris*), ground nut (*Arachis hypogea*) and root crops, namely cassava (*Manihot esculenta Cranz*), and sweet potato (*Ipomea batatas*).

The extension networks promoted agronomic practices and technologies that were not significantly above the financial capacity of the producers, especially subsistence farmers. When DNDR was established in 1987, it was assumed that the use of external inputs would be appropriate for commercial farms that had mechanization and support facilities such as irrigation, drainage and storage systems. For the family sector, extensionists focused on improved technology and crop management practices for the principal food crops.

Extension workers advised farmers on the following:

- Recommended time of seeding;
- Spacing for different crops (in monoculture);
- Thinning 1 or 2 plants per hole;
- Timely weeding;
- Recommended time of harvesting;
- Use of locally made organic insecticides for grain and seed conservation; and,
- Rotation or intercropping with specific cereals and legumes with advantages to the crops and soil.

## Building Extension Capacity

Public extension was created during a period of an acute scarcity of qualified technicians in agriculture. State farms, cooperatives and agricultural projects had formerly employed most of the technicians and foremen who formed the initial cadre of public extension workers. The foremen were selected from among capable and experienced farmers and given practical training to prepare them to act as diffusers of basic technical knowledge and practices. Each was responsible for at least one village and about 300 up to 400 small-scale producers (Gonçalves 1992).

In 1987, the Ministry of Agriculture offered the first pre-admission extension course to seventy-one technicians. The majority of the technicians had certificate level education but some had a lower level of education. The creation of DNDR helped upgrade human resources in the extension service. Gonçalves (1992) defines field extensionists as multi-purpose technicians with a minimum of certificate level and a graduate of a pre-admission training course offered by the Ministry of Agriculture. It became obvious that the minimum level of academic education needed to be elevated to improve staff capability and there was a need to develop a career ladder for extensionists. The following job categories were adopted for frontline extension staff: field extensionist, subject matter specialist, extension supervisor and subject matter supervisor.

Because of the low academic level and skills of the extensionists during the start-up phase of public extension, in-service training programs were developed to strengthen the competence of the public extension. From 1989 to 1992, about 10 to 20 percent of DNDR's budget was allocated to training. Three types of in-service training were defined as a priority when the DNDR was established:

- *Pre-admission.* Pre admission extension courses of about 60 days covered basic theoretical knowledge of the philosophy, objectives, organizational structure and functions of the public extension service and included training in the rural participatory approach (RPA). The initial training was used to screen and select future extensionists. About 80 to 90 percent of the "graduates" of pre-admission courses were hired by the public extension services.

- *Refresher courses.* These courses were of importance to specialists, managers, subject matter specialists, supervisors and extensionists because they helped update human capital throughout the professional career of the technicians.

- *Career advancement.* Halim and Mozahar (1997) contend that academic training increases the knowledge, ability and capacity of extension workers in general and prepares them for greater responsibility and higher positions in the organization. Malone (1984) argues that extension organizations should encourage extension agents to pursue academic training because technicians and managers will derive job satisfaction, stability of employment and increase their effectiveness and the efficiency of the organization. DNER emphasizes the importance of this type of training particularly from diploma to B.Sc. level.

## Financing Public Extension: The Role of External Partners

In Mozambique and many other African countries, donors have financed public extension heavily for many years. Also, the long-standing donor practice of using autonomous projects to implement extension projects makes it difficult to estimate the total value of external funding for extension in Mozambique from 1987 to 1997. However with the advent of the National Agricultural Sector Development Program (PROAGRI) in 1998, this type of information is now readily available from donors on an annual basis. The major sources of external finance for extension from 1987 to 1992 were: FAO; IFAD; UNICEF; DANIDA; GTZ and the Government of Mozambique through the then Agricultural and Rural Development Fund (FFADR).

FAO and UNDP provided initial institutional support to the central DNDR and five districts (Xai-Xai, Maxixe, Inhambane, Pemba-Metuge and Lichinga) from 1989 to 1993. Managed by a coordination unit, the FAO project co-financed transport and field equipment as well as the operational costs of the extension networks in the districts mentioned above.

UNICEF supported extension activities from 1989 to 1996 through integrated rural development projects. This support helped establish and strengthen some extension networks such as Ile and Namacurra (Zambezia province), Mossurize and Barue (Manica province), Massinga and Panda (Inhambane province). The co-financing by UNICEF included transport, field equipment, some agricultural inputs such as improved seeds, cassava cuttings, and the operating expenses of extensionists. UNICEF at the provincial level such as Zambezia and Manica directly managed the projects.

IFAD was one of the early partners of DNDR beginning in 1989. IFAD provided operating funds and a capital budget, which was used to purchase vehicles and field equipment. The financial support by IFAD was processed through the former Banco Popular de Desenvolvimento (BPD). At the level of the Ministry of Agriculture, the Directorate of Agricultural Economics monitored the utilization of funds by DNDR and joint IFAD and DNDR missions made periodic visits to extension sites.

In the early 1990s nearly all donor support was concentrated at the central DNDR office. However, DANIDA moved quickly to support provincial and district levels. DANIDA supported public extension from 1989 to 1998 and it was one of the pioneers in establishing project coordination units at the provincial level within the Provincial Directorate of Agriculture. DANIDA provided two forms of technical assistance: one was through a team of management and technical assistance in Tete province (DANIDA 2002a) and the other was through contracting (outsourcing) to a Danish NGO–IBIS for the provision of technical assistance to Nicoadala district in Zambezia province using public extension workers (insourcing).

GTZ has co-financed some public extension activities in Manica Province and Sofala Province. The former Mozambican Agricultural and Rural Development Fund (FFADR) played an important role in strengthening public extension, particularly during the first six years of its operation. The fund provided financial support to pay the salaries of about 70 percent of the extensionists on contract.

### Agricultural Production Support Services

When public extension was established in 1987, the complementary agricultural support services were quite weak and they were deeply involved in supporting large-scale state farms and cooperatives. The agricultural support services in Mozambique can be divided into six categories:

■ Agricultural Research Services

The National Institute of Agronomic Research (INIA), has four research stations and three agronomic posts (secondary level stations) throughout the country. However, since the post independence agricultural development strategy focused on large state farms, INIA's research program was also directed to large-scale farms. One of INIA's main contributions during the 1987–92 periods was the development and release of improved maize and rice varieties. In animal research, there were three research stations, two in the south and one in the central region of the country.

■ Support Services for Field Operations

Labor is one of the major constraints on Mozambican agriculture. Although subsistence agriculture relies heavily on family labor, some semi-subsistence farmers are in a position to hire labor for some activities, particularly for soil preparation and harvesting such as rice in the Chokwe irrigation perimeter (about 24,000 ha). The Mecanagro State Enterprise (1982–93) was established in all provinces as the main provider of water pumps; tractors and vans; and irrigation systems, agro-industries and stores.

■ Agricultural Inputs and Equipment Services

During the first five years of public extension (1987 to 1992), SEMOC (former Mozambican and Swedish JVC) was the only seed company operating in the country and it focused on selling improved open pollinated varieties (OPVs) of maize and improved varieties of rice, beans, and cowpeas. Two public companies, namely ENACOMO E.E. and BOROR, were established in almost all the provincial capitals to sell fertilizer and pesticides mainly to state and private farms. Foreign companies were active in selling agricultural tools (hoes, machetes, and axes) that were mainly distributed through humanitarian assistance programs.

■ Agricultural Training

The National Agricultural Training Center (CFA) was established in 1988 (BR, Series 1, January, 1987) in Maputo, a year before the installation of Provincial Agricultural Training Centers (CPFA) in all ten Provinces of the country. The center had a mandate to train extensionists, groups of farmers as well as district administrators and other interested people.

■ Marketing and Processing

AGRICOM State Enterprise (1983–92) promoted the production and marketing of various commodities such as cereals (maize and rice) and legumes (groundnuts and beans). The terms of exchange included cash payments to farmers as well as bartering farm commodities for agricultural tools and other items. With representation in all the ten provinces, the Enterprise had a large network of rural warehouses. The Enterprise was replaced by the Cereal Institute of Mozambique (ICM) in 1994 and given the same mandate but it was independent of the government. During the first five years of the public extension, industrial agro-processing included five rice processing factories, three grinding mills, two tomato processing factories and three cotton processing factories in the north. These basic agro-industries were almost all owned by the government until the early 1990s. With the exception of the cotton and cashew processing factories, the others were mainly located in the south and central regions of the country.

## Private Extension

Private extension emerged in 1990 and 1991 in the northern region with the goal of expanding cotton production, which had fallen with the collapse of state farms in the second half of 1980s. Private extension emerged in the provinces of Nampula, Cabo-Delgado and Niassa, main producers of cotton and tobacco. Private firms formed Joint Venture Companies (JVCs) in large areas (districts) previously farmed by state cotton enterprises. The JVCs developed a voluntary contractual partnership between farmers and concessionaires who provide seeds and pesticides to smallholders growing the chosen commodity on contract. The concessionaires also provided technical assistance to small-scale farms through "field monitors" as well as bags at harvest time. The small scale farmers signed contracts to sell their cotton to the respective concessionaires for processing and export. Three large private cotton companies introduced private extension on concessions provided by the State through the Cotton Institute of Mozambique (IAM). The following JVCs developed cotton extension programs: LOMACO (Lonrho-Mozambique Agro-Industrial Company), SAMO (Cotton Society of Monapo-Nampula), SAN (Cotton

The master plan, assumed that public extension would consist of 36 extension networks composed of about 700 extensionists in 52 of the 128 districts in the country. Moreover, the master plan was forthright in arguing that increasing the density of public extension would require a major government commitment to seek additional external assistance to finance the operating cost as well as housing, vehicles and motorcycles for extension staff. The extension master plan also assumed that the government's contribution to public extension could gradually be reduced over time because farmers, farm organizations and the private sector would eventually pay some of the user costs.

The 1994 extension strategy and the 1995 draft extension master plan laid out five central features of public extension:

- *geographic concentration:* the vision of operating in about half of the districts of the country to achieve rapid economic growth
- *agro-ecology:* give priority to high potential areas that offer the best possibility of a rapid increase in production
- *two approaches:* general extension with emphasis on food crops and commodity extension focusing on cotton, sunflower, sesame and cashew nut.
- *decentralization:* devolve responsibility for the operation of networks to the provincial service of extension (SPERs), and,
- *pluralism:* long term perspective of increased private sector extension, private enterprises and NGOs in the provision of extension services.

## The NGO Transition from Humanitarian Aid to Development

The NGOs scaled up their operations in 1993–94 and transformed themselves from providers of humanitarian assistance to agents of development. The number of international NGOs increased from thirty in 1994 to sixty-seven in the 1997–98 agricultural season, covering some forty of the one hundred and twenty-eight districts in the country (DNER M&E Surveys 1994, 1997). In the beginning, most NGOs focused on providing agricultural extension with emphasis on food crops and animal restocking, particularly poultry and goats. But the philosophies, objectives, approaches and methodologies of NGOs varied considerably. The rapid entry of NGOs into agricultural extension after peace was declared is attributed to the following factors:

- The political leadership of Mozambique acknowledged the need to invest in agriculture because several million families were dependent upon agriculture for their food security and the food security of Mozambique.
- The willingness of donors to finance agricultural development and extension projects.
- The credibility and encouragement that NGOs enjoyed from donors as valid actors in both humanitarian assistance as well as in agricultural and rural development programs.
- The government's decision to promote a pluralistic extension delivery system as a strategy to spread extension coverage and promote effectiveness and competitiveness.

However, the case for NGOs as effective development agents was not based on their performance and achievements in rural areas of Mozambique. Rather, the government viewed NGOs as a new source of private and public funding for development programs because many of the traditional multilateral and bilateral donors believed that NGOs were more efficient, effective and flexible than many public extension services (Edwards 2002; World Bank 2003). These beliefs guided the decisions of many donors to offer contracts to NGOs to implement development projects, including the provision of extension assistance. Also, the government used the funds and technical capacity of donors to extend agricultural extension to many rural areas where public extension was not operating. The principal extension activity of many of the NGOs was the introduction of new crop varieties and helping farmers rebuild their livestock herds that had been decimated during the Civil War.

- ■ Characteristics of NGO Extension Programs

To date most NGOs involved in agricultural extension and related activities have been international NGOs. The emergence of national NGOs is a recent development because historically the Government has been a regulator, controller and provider of agricultural services and it did not endorse the spread of international and local NGOs (Kanji et al. 2002). However, by the late 1980s, several dozen international NGOs were authorized to help deliver emergency humanitarian assistance throughout the country.

Numerous international NGOs provided humanitarian assistance to Mozambique during the Civil War in the late eighties and early nineties until peace was declared in 1992. Starting in 1993, many international NGOs shifted to the implementation of extension, rural development and health projects. For example, in 1985 DANIDA helped finance an emergency activity to supply agricultural inputs in Tete province. But, over time, the project evolved into an activity supporting the establishment of an agricultural extension service for smallholders (DANIDA 2002b).

Farmer participation was and is still used by many NGOs as a means of helping mobilize funds from donors and as an aid in the implementation of project activities. In fact, many NGOs devote more attention to community participation as the ultimate goal rather than as a tool to pursue agricultural development. Most NGOs have promoted the involvement of "animators" and community members. But in general, community development agents often lack academic preparation and experience to generate change within their communities. Finally, some NGOs have provided free bicycles, radios, and agricultural implements as a means of ensuring the "collaboration" of local actors. Although gifts can help achieve short term goals, the medium-and long-term effects are often debilitating because they distort the incentive structure and impede the emergence of normal market forces for credit and seed distribution systems.

The economics of NGO extension in Mozambique is an unknown quantity. Even if the cost per farmer were known, it would still be necessary to compare the costs with the benefits (Evenson 1986, 2001). Also, it would be helpful to know how much farmers would be willing to contribute to finance extension services. Most evaluations of NGOs have historically been prepared for donors and they frequently have not been shared with public extension managers.

The following can be mentioned as the main achievements of NGOs:

- Increase in geographical extension coverage and farmers reached,
- Creation of job opportunities for agricultural technicians, including highly qualified staff in rural areas,
- Promotion of learning by doing extension within pluralistic delivery system
- Diversification of extension activities (food security, farmers organization, market support, agricultural advocacy, HIV/AIDS in agriculture, etc.)

However, from 1993 to 1997, most NGOs took pains to keep donors informed of their problems and progress, but most did little to exchange programmatic ideas and financial information with public extension managers. This was disturbing because the three extension service providers have the same goal in mind: to serve small-scale farms and help speed the transformation of agriculture into an engine of economic, and equitable growth. Likewise, agricultural districts and provincial authorities received little information during this period about NGOs' extension programs or projects. Although much was accomplished during PROAGRI 1, there is still more that can be done to increase the connectivity between public, private and NGO extension in Mozambique.

■ Modification of the T&V Extension Model

DNER decided to modify the T&V system in order to adapt it to Mozambican conditions and the different environments in the extension networks. Basically two changes were made. First, instead of requiring extensionists to meet with contact farmers (one per village), they were directed to work with groups of farmers. Second, the rigid timetable of meeting every fifteen days was removed, and extensionists were allowed to develop more flexible meeting times, usually quite frequently during the growing season.

The objective of working with farmer groups was to increase the coverage of the service in terms of number of farmers per field extension worker, to expand the flow of information between groups of farmers and increase the possibility of identifying more talented farmers or those who would undertake risks in experimenting with new technologies. Each extensionist had to work with eight to sixteen groups with an average of 225 farmers per extension worker.

However, the number of farmers per extensionist varied according to population density, settlement pattern, access to roads, availability of transport, soil relief and physical characteristics that might facilitate or impede the mobility of extensionists, especially during the rainy season and taking into consideration that bicycle is the main means of transport of public extensionists. The adoption of flexibility as an operating norm was designed to reduce the negative effects surrounding pre-established meetings between extensionists, farmers, field supervisors and SMSs as well as rationalizing financial and material resources.

**Expansion of Public Extension**

The period from 1993 to 1997 was marked by an increase in the geographical coverage (especially in Nampula and Cabo-Delgado provinces) and institutional consolidation of public extension from forty extension networks (districts) in 1992 to forty-nine networks in 1997. The intensity of service delivery was also increased during this period (table 2). Much of this expansion in coverage and increase in intensity was facilitated by the arrival of three new international partners: the World Bank helped expand the area covered while the FAO's special program for food security and Sasakawa Global 2000 helped to intensify the delivery of services (Haag 2000). These new partners provided funding to help increase the size, coverage and intensity of the entire public extension service by including funds for vehicles, bicycles, motorbikes and field equipment for extension technicians. Starting in 1995, public extension began to

**Table 2.** Expansion of Public Extension Networks, 1993–97

| PROVINCE | EXTENSION DISTRICTS | |
| --- | --- | --- |
| | 1993 | 1997 |
| MAPUTO | Boane, Matutuine | Boane, Matutuine |
| GAZA | Xai-Xai, Chibuto, Bilene, Manjacaze | Xai-Xai, Chibuto, Bilene, Manjacaze |
| INHAMBANE | Panda, Massing a Maxixe, Jangamo, Inhambane, Morrumbene | Panda, Massinga, Homoine, Inhassoro, Vilanculo, Govouro |
| SOFALA | Dondo, Nhamatanda, Buzi | Dondo, Nhamatanda, Buzi, Gorongosa |
| MANICA | Sussundenga, Gondola, Manica, Mossurize, Barue | Sussundenga, Gondola, Manica, Mossurize, Barue |
| TETE | Moatize, Angonia, Tsangano | Moatize, Angonia, Tsangano |
| ZAMBEZIA | Nicoadala, Ile, Namacura, Alto Molocue, Mocuba | Nicoadala, Ile, Namacurra, Alto Molocue, Mocuba |
| NAMPULA | Ribaue, Malema, Angoche, Meconta | Ribaue, Malema, Angoche, Meconta, Monapo, Muecate, Erate, Lalaua, Namapa, Mecuburi |
| NIASSA | Sanga, Lichinga | Mandimba, Sanga, Lichinga |
| CABO-DELGADO | Pemba-Metuge, Montepuez, Mueda, Namuno, Chuire | Pemba-Metuge, Montepuez, Mueda, Namuno, Chuire, Nangade, Muidumbe |
| *Total* | *39* | *49* |

disseminate technological packages (improved seeds, inorganic fertilizers and later herbicides) for cereals such as maize and rice.

World Bank support to public extension through the Agricultural Rehabilitation and Agricultural Services Rehabilitation and Development Projects (PRDA and PRDSA)—was negotiated over the 1991–92 period and it became effective in December 1993 (World Bank 2001). World Bank support to public extension was decisive in adding new extension networks in four provinces: Nampula, Cabo-Delgado, Gaza, and Inhambane (World Bank 2000, 2001). The World Bank also financed frequent field visits by international specialists to study the operation of extension networks, particularly those funded by the Bank. Many of the Bank evaluators of DNER visited the field for a brief period of time and then criticized the weak and irrelevant extension messages. However, many of the Bank specialists failed to present concrete proposals on how to solve these problems. In fact, the periodic evaluators can be described as using the "expert judgment" approach, in which the specialists read reports, interviewed some extensionists; and, after brief field visits, produced their findings and recommendations. But these frequent visits and evaluations of the performance of DNER extensionists were not always carried out in a systematic and useful manner. The same can be said about the evaluation of technology adoption because many of the simple technology messages are still relevant. For example, because of low fertility of most soils throughout the country, one of the principal reasons for low yields in the family sector is low plant population density per unit area. This is aggravated by the practice of putting three or four seeds per hole and seeding randomly (Gemo 2001). The technical recommendations of adequate plant population combined with good soil management (intercropping, rotation, minimum tillage) are still relevant.

SG 2000 is an international NGO committed to accelerating agricultural development in Africa. In 1995, SG 2000 opened an office in the National Directorate of Rural Extension in Maputo. In retrospect, the decision to set up an office within DNER in Maputo and reinforce extension at all levels, sent a powerful signal to the then Ministry of Agriculture and Fisheries (MAP) and to the donor community that a strong and pluralistic extension system had an important role to play in technology transfer. The SG 2000 project had three goals. The overarching goal was to develop technology packages that could help family farms double or triple the yields of staple food crops. Second, SG 2000 provided limited but critical budget support to pay some of DNER's operational costs such as, transport and field equipment while always stressing the need for field impact—i.e., increasing crop yields on the fields of farmers. Third, SG 2000 assumed that promoting the use of external inputs (pesticides, inorganic fertilizer and improved seeds) on demonstration plots on the fields of subsistence farmers would have a demonstration effect and expand the use of external inputs by an emerging sub set of farms called commercial smallholders.

SG 2000's main field program consisted of conducting carefully designed demonstration plots on the fields of farmers covering a wide array of food crops in all provinces (Haag 2000). All three types of extension providers focused the partnership between the public extension service and SG 2000 on the development of food crop packages for smallholders that could be disseminated by all three extension providers.[1]

The SG 2000 field program was launched in the 1995–96 growing season by planting demonstration maize and rice plots on the fields of forty farmers. Maize and rice were chosen because they were traditional food staples and they had benefited from past research. Mozambique has a large potential to produce rice.[2] The initial SG 2000 demonstration plots were 0.5 hectares in size. The use of larger than normal demonstration plots was based on the assumption that farmers would evaluate the dramatic difference in production between subsistence yields and those of the SG 2000 package and decide to adopt the new package during the following year.

During the second phase from 1993 to 1997, DNER and SG 2000 diffused improved open-pollinated maize varieties (Manica SR and Matuba), groundnut (Natal common and Makulo Red), cowpea (IT 18) and rice (ITA 312 and C4 63). DNER extensionists also diffused improved varieties of horticultural crops to farmers around the provincial capitals of Gaza (Xai Xai), Inhambane (Inhambane and Maxixe), Cabo-Delgado (Pemba Metuge district), and Maputo (Boane and Marracuene districts).

The first two agricultural seasons were a challenge to the SG 2000 program because many NGOs and, to some extent, the ministry of agriculture, continued to distribute free certified seed to farmers displaced by the war. This reduced the availability of certified seed in rural markets because the then sole seed company (SEMOC, Lda) was able to sell its entire seed stock to humanitarian agencies.

In 2001–2, DNER/SG 2000 planted 8,986 demonstration plots of 14 different crops in ten provinces. Maize represented about 40 percent of the plots. The SG 2000 program summed up its 8-year experience by noting that because subsistence farmers have shown that they can dramatically increase yields with external inputs, the challenge ahead is as follows: "The major agricultural intensification challenge remains the strengthening of the entire input supply system and the provision of reasonable output prices" (Sasakawa Africa 2002.)

Researchers, extension workers and policymakers, should carefully study the experience of the SG 2000 program in Mozambique because it has encouraged farmers to adopt a package of purchased inputs. This is an important question because many donors also encourage farmers to adopt the entire package. Another question is whether the SG 2000 package is profitable to smallholders on a recurring basis and at an accepted level of risk. To date there are only two economic studies of the SG 2000 program in Mozambique. The first is Mucavale's study of the economics of smallholder rice production in Bilene-Macia District. Mucavele (2000) analyzed the economics of the rice package and concluded that rice was viable in the south of the country, provided smallholders can generate a minimum yield of 3.5 tons/ha, and secure 2001 prices for their rice, certified seed, inorganic fertilizers, and herbicides. The second is a three year study of the improved smallholder maize production packages in Nampula and Manica provinces. Howard et al. (1998), studied the 1996-97 season and found that the SG 2000 package did increase yields of maize substantially, but the yields were highly variable. Also, because of high input costs and low maize prices at harvest time, some of the surveyed farmers lost money from their investment in the maize package. The survey was continued in 1997–98 season and maize yields were affected by late delivery of inputs, inadequate extension assistance and other factors (Howard et al. 2000). The study was carried out for a third season (1999–2000) and one of the important results was the need to move away from blanket fertilizer recommendations to recommendations geared more specifically to different soils and economic capacities of farmers (Howard et al. 2002a).[3] This type of study should be carried out again in the near future because it can provide feedback from farmers to SG 2000, INIA, the three extension providers and donors and it can be used to develop best practices for farmers growing maize.[4]

## Private Extension Experiments

From 1993 to 1998 the climate of peace enabled private companies and JVCs to expand cotton production and offer private extension assistance to small-scale farms growing mainly cotton under contract. The reduction of government expenditures on national security permitted government funds to be redirected to finance services to promote the production and processing of cotton. However, the average FOB price for export of prime cotton in Mozambique declined from US$1,443 per ton in 1993–94 to US$1,021 in 1997–98, a reduction of 25 percent in four years (Boughton et al. 2002). In spite of this sharp decline, the number of companies registered to grow and commercialize cotton had increased during this period, partially as a result of the new government policy of offering a guaranteed minimum producer price for cotton and later through negotiation of establishing prices between government, private companies and farmer organizations.

### NOTES

1. But the use of a package of improved seeds, inorganic fertilizers, and insecticides was not a new innovation in Mozambique. Smallholders producing cotton on contract used external inputs starting in the early 1990s.
2. Mozambique is cultivating around 200,000 hectares of rice out of a potential area of about 900,000 hectares suitable for rice. Rice imports are currently running about US$20 to 40 million per year.
3. There is evidence that farmers typically select one or two components of a recommended package for testing on their farms and then adopting the most profitable components in a gradient (Walker 1981) or stepwise approach (Byerlee and Polanco 1986).
4. See Matsumoto, Plucknet, and Takase (2003) for an evaluation of the Sasakawa Global 2000 Program in Mozambique.

# CHAPTER 5

# The PROAGRI Period: The First Extension Master Plan, Decentralization, and Outsourcing Extension: 1999–2004

## PROAGRI: 1999–2004

Soon after peace was declared in 1992, the Ministry of Agriculture decided to shift gears and undertake badly needed institutional reforms to complement the policy reforms. To address the freewheeling donor behavior during the rehabilitation period, the government placed all UNDP projects under the Ministry of Agriculture in 1993 and used UNDP support to build the managerial and technical capacity to pursue a sectoral approach to agricultural decision-making and donor coordination. This period was called Pre-program preparation (1992–94). After elections in 1994, the Ministry of Agriculture started to work on the preparation of PROAGRI (the National Program for Agricultural Development). PROAGRI (1998) was prepared because the Ministry of Agriculture found itself in a position throughout the nineties where its programs were being supported by "a confusing and an uncoordinated array of donor initiatives" (World Bank 1999). The government summarized its mixed experience with donor projects in the 1990s as follows:

The MAP (Ministry of Agriculture and Fisheries) has been carrying out investments using external funds made available through projects in which the government contribution stood below 10 percent of the global amounts. The projects are very often designed and implemented by donors, while the Government stands by as a mere observer or as a passive recipient within the chain of decisions regarding those projects. This situation has led to the lack of continuity of the projects and the weakening of the MAP itself, as the best staff have been attracted to work for the projects which offer better incentives and working conditions. (PROAGRI 1998)

Mozambique introduced PROAGRI to coordinate pooled donor investments in the agricultural sector (PROAGRI 1998); European Commission 1998). The key to donor endorsement was a set of basic principles. PROAGRI's basic principles can be regarded as part of the GOM policy framework for the agricultural sector: poverty alleviation, decentralization and empowerment, good governance, environmental and social sustainability, and market-oriented policy. In 1998, donors reviewed the PROAGRI (sector investment program) and endorsed its three major sub programs:

- Institutional development to improve the structure of the Ministry of Agriculture, strengthen the operations of the ministry at both central and provincial levels, and develop policy analysis capability;
- Strengthen agricultural support services—livestock, support to agricultural production, research, and extension. (Increasing farmer participation and developing a more pluralistic extension service); and
- Improve natural resource management (forestry, irrigation and land).

PROAGRI is basically a public investment program in agriculture that is supported by pooled funding by a number of donors, including the World Bank, IFAD, DANIDA, EU, USAID, AuAID, Holland, Italy, Ireland, DFID, and Finland. PROAGRI had an estimated budget of US$205 million for a period of five years (1998–2003). PROAGRI is designed to improve public agricultural services through institutional reforms of the Ministry of

Agriculture and agricultural research (PROAGRI 2000, 2001, 2001a; World Bank 2004, 484–85).

PROAGRI includes support for eight activities: extension, research, livestock, land, irrigation, institutional reforms, forestry, and wildlife. Public extension and research are considered to be pillars of PROAGRI. In 2003, there were eighteen cooperating partners (donors) and eleven of the eighteen contributed funds to a Common Flow of Funds Mechanism to finance all eight components of PROAGRI. The participating partners (donors) financed about US$35.3 million (84 percent) of PROAGRI's budget of US$42 million in 2003 (PROAGRI 2002a). PROAGRI has made substantial progress but donors raised a number of reservations and some key donors delayed their annual contribution until late in 2004.

## The First Extension Master Plan

In 1997, the public extension service prepared the first Extension Master Plan covering 1998 to 2003 (DNER 1997). The plan includes a number of innovations. First, the master plan adopted a unified extension program involving crop production, livestock and natural resource management. Second, the Plan stated that public extension would be operating in a maximum of fifty-two districts organized in thirty-six extension network areas by 2003 (one extension network may include from one to three districts). Third, the plan calls for functional partnerships between public and private extension services, including the development of public contracts with other service providers ("outsourcing") and the use of public extension staff by NGOs (in sourcing) to deliver extension services to farmers. Fourth, it explicitly identified the necessary resources for an effective national public extension system and makes an appeal for increased funding from external partners. Finally, the plan called for increased connectivity with other institutions such as research, agricultural service and marketing institutions; and mentioned the possibility of cost recovery from farmers served by public extension (Eicher 2002, 2004).

## Expanded Geographical Coverage of the Master Plan

The geographical coverage of the first master plan included thirty-six extension network areas covering parts of fifty-two districts in all ten provinces in the country (DNER 1997). DNER expanded extension coverage in fourteen new districts during the first master plan from 1999 to 2004. Table 3 shows that public extension was operating in sixty-six districts and all ten provinces in 2004. The new districts were selected through intensive consultations with provinces according to the following criteria: potential to increase agricultural production with available technology, rural population density, ease of road access, existing extension activities, research coverage and other support services. By the end of 2004, the extension service was assumed to cover about 25 percent of all farm families.

## Unified Extension

Bagchee (1994) contends that the unification of extension has one over-reaching goal of rationalizing resources by bringing together crop, livestock and forestry extension into a single force at the field level. In Mozambique, unified extension started in the 1998–99 agricultural season, and it involves the collaboration and coordination of activities among the extension service and other Ministry of Agriculture services, such as livestock, forestry, and, to a lesser degree, irrigation. The development of a unified extension approach is based on the integration of subject matter specialists (SMSs) of agriculture, livestock and natural resource conservation into the extension networks and the provincial level (DNER 1997a, 1997c). At the extension network level, most of the SMSs have a diploma while those at the provincial level have B.Sc. degrees.

The necessary conditions for successful unified extension are:

- A single front of multipurpose extensionists in the field assisted by experienced SMSs, equipped and integrated into the extension networks
- Strong linkages between farmers, extension and research

**Table 3.** DNER: District Coverage, 2004

| PROVINCE | DISTRICTS WITH EXTENSIONISTS | NUMBER OF DISTRICTS | |
|---|---|---|---|
| | | PLANNED 1992 | OPERATING 2004 |
| MAPUTO | Boane, Matutuine, Magude, Moamba, Manhica, Namaacha | 4 | 6 |
| GAZA | Chokwe, Xai-Xai, Bilene, Manjagaze, Chibuto | 5 | 5 |
| INHAMBANE | Massinga, Morrumbene, Homoine, Panda, Inharrime, Jangamo | 6 | 6 |
| SOFALA | Buzi, Nhamatanda, Dondo, Gorongoza,Cheba, Maringue, Mwanza, Caia, Chibobova | 4 | 9 |
| MANICA | Sussundenga, Gondola, Manica, Mossurize, Barue, Macossa | 5 | 6 |
| TETE | Angonia, Tsangano, Moatize, Changara, Cahora Bassa | 4 | 5 |
| ZAMBEZIA | Nicoadala, Mocuba, Alto-Molocue, Ile, Namacura, Pebane | 6 | 6 |
| NAMPULA | Nampula, Mecuburi, Muecate, Ribaue, Malema, Namapa, Monapo, Meconta, Angoche, Mogovolas, Balama | 9 | 11 |
| CABO-DELGADO | Montepuez, Balama, Namuno, Chiure, Mueda, Muidumbe, Nagade | 7 | 7 |
| NIASSA | Lichinga, Sanga, Majune, Cuamba, Mandimba | 2 | 5 |
| *Total* | | 52 | 66 |

*Source*: DNER 2004.

- Joint planning and coordinated implementation of extension activities among the extension services and, above all, the livestock and forestry services. The irrigation and drainage component, in spite of its enormous importance in drought situations and flooding, was not included in the unification plan.
- Joint monitoring and evaluation of activities of different services within unified extension. The provincial and central SMSs were considered to be critical in ensuring that last two conditions are met.

In crop production, the marriage between the SMSs of plant production and protection was assumed to improve the performance of extensionists. Turning to livestock, the extension service addressed the main livestock diseases and introduced feed management and production practices. Plans were also made to accelerate the training of community development agents on how to vaccinate chickens against Newcastle disease (dos Anjos et al. 2001) and provide mineral blocks for cattle to stimulate their appetite in areas such as the highlands of Angonia in Tete province. To summarize, the implementation of the unified system of extension from 1999 to 2004 is behind schedule. The Livestock Service is further along than other services because it has about 62 percent of the SMSs necessary at the extension network areas and about 90 percent at the provincial level. The joint planning and implementation of activities between extension, crop production and livestock extension have reached a satisfactory working level. But this varies in the ten provinces of the country.

The experience to date shows that provincial directors of agriculture can play an important role in promoting collaboration among the provincial extension and livestock, forestry, and irrigation services. However, in natural resources management, comparatively little has been achieved. In the year 2000, the National Directorate of Forestry and Wildlife (DNFFB) allocated SMSs to the provincial and district levels for the entire country but only about 30 percent of the total required for extension networks.

The partnership between extension and the irrigation and drainage services is off to a slow start. Under the "Special Programme for Food Security (SPFS)," FAO provided some financial support for the construction of two pilot irrigation systems (5 to 8 hectares) that are to be managed by communities. The role of extension is to provide technical assistance in the production and commercialization of the irrigated crops. However, this is a new experience. Two schemes were developed in two provinces in 2002. In addition, FAO and IFAD have supported the introduction of about 650 treadle pumps in Sofala and Niassa provinces through extension networks. Although there are some unanswered technical and logistical problems, treadle pumps are now viewed as an alternative for smallholders facing frequent drought in the central and southern regions of the country. Malawi has had a good experience with thousands of treadle pumps, which cost about US$125 per pump (in

Mozambique). Each pump has the potential of irrigating 0.5 ha. But little is known about the economics of irrigation in Mozambique.

In summary, if unified extension is to continue as the main approach of public extension, work remains to be done to make it more cohesive, and effective especially in terms of reducing the staff turnover, organizational setup and placement of the SMSs and coordination between the extension and other services within the then MADER (Ye et al. 2003). Improved and continuous training of extensionists will be necessary to improve joint planning, implementation and M&E between the services involved.

### Progressive Decentralization

The third stage in the evolution of public extension from 1999–2004 occurred as part of the general reform of the entire public sector to achieve greater efficiency and effectiveness. In Mozambique, there is a lively debate on the necessity of decentralization of planning and budgeting and devolving the responsibility for implementing extension to the district level. Currently many academics and some donors are urging greater decentralizing of the responsibility for and the management of extension to the provincial, district and ultimately community levels. But there is little guidance from academic researchers on how to institutionalize extension at the community level and encourage farmers to demand accountability of local extensionists.

By 2003, nearly 65 to 70 percent of the total budget of public extension was directly managed at the provincial level. Until 1997, all financial resources were channeled through the central government, with the exception of DANIDA's direct financing of extension in two provinces (Zambezia and Tete), GTZ financing for (Manica province) and EEC financing for Inhambane province.[1] The transport of agricultural inputs for field demonstrations has been centralized and executed by project management units. The current apprenticeship of public extension can be viewed as an experiment in decentralization to the provinces (Manor 1998).

Mozambique has made substantial progress in transferring budget and decision power to the provincial level. The 30 to 35 percent of total public extension budget that is managed at the central level is used to finance activities such as training and the procurement of specialized equipment for extension staff at the provincial and district levels and financing supervision missions. Most of the procurement of goods and services has been transferred to the provinces.

Without a doubt, there are many challenges surrounding decentralization. The resolution of these will provide guidance for further decentralization. To be sure, there has been notable institutional strengthening over the past seventeen years of public extension. The extensionists, SMSs, and supervisors, for example, are based in the field and the provincial services are established and functioning. But most provincial services of extension only have one to two B.Sc. level graduates and the rest of the staff have diplomas or certificates. Moreover, there is not a transparent plan to increase the formal training of technicians and develop career ladders and incentives to retain extension workers for a 20- to 30-year career in DNER. In fact, experienced extension staff at the network and provincial levels are often transferred to other services within the Ministry of Agriculture. For example, about 40 percent of the district agricultural directors appointed in the last five years have been from extension. The distribution of the annual budget and the allocation of funds at the provincial level between extension and other services is still based on subjective and, in some cases, on equal distribution among the various departments. A better allocation of resources needs to be based on clearly defined short and long-term priorities among the different departments. To summarize, there is a large gap between the theory and practice of decentralization. There is an urgent need for socioeconomic research on how to devolve extension to districts and ensure accountability.

## Radio and Mass Communication

The use of mass media communication has increased in importance in public extension. Today, radio is the most utilized means of communication to reach farmers and rural communities in Mozambique. In fact, the purchase of a radio or a bicycle is one of the first signs of increased incomes by rural families. Extension programs in local languages are transmitted by radio broadcasts in the provinces, normally early in the morning or early evening.

The radio has also been used extensively in extension campaigns. For example, during the land preparation period, extensionists use radio to appeal to farmers to guard against uncontrolled bush burning, a serious problem in the country. When there is a drought or flood forecast, the radio is critical in providing emergency advice to rural communities. The radio is also used to make farmers aware of when and how to pursue pruning and chemical treatment of cashew trees as well as the vaccination of chickens against Newcastle disease. Oídium is one of the main diseases causing low productivity of about 26 million cashew nut trees belonging to about 40 percent of the family sector. Newcastle is responsible for the death of 50 to 80 percent of chickens, particularly in the family sector (dos Anjos et al. 2001).

## Reinforcement of Research, Extension, and Marketing Linkages

The challenge for Mozambique is to develop a system of interactive agricultural institutions, which communicate, cooperate and reinforce each other to achieve the shared goal of increasing agricultural productivity and driving down real (inflation adjusted) food prices over time (Bonnen 1998). Unfortunately the linkages between extension, research and marketing have not improved significantly over the 1999–2004 period. There are three main reasons for this impasse. The first is that although the research and extension services are highly complementary, they continue to work on their own agendas and priorities. The lack of effective functional linkages between extension and research is part of an environment where there is a fragmented approach to decision-making and implementing decisions. In order to overcome this problem, the first Joint National Meeting of Research and Extension that was held in May 2003 in Lichinga (Niassa Province), approved an action plan for the coming five years that addresses these crucial issues. The second reason for the extension/ research impasse is the fact that both services have serious funding and human capital constraints. For example, in the last five years, about 65 to 75 percent of the annual budget directly allocated to extension has been used to pay staff salaries. The third reason is there is not a transparent "career ladder" that provides training, and incentives to build a cadre of highly committed professionals in both extension and research who are on a particular job for long enough to develop contacts and trust with professionals in other services. There is a dearth of information on career pathways for extensionists in the public, NGO and private arenas and a lack of information on how to advance over time.

Within the National Agricultural Development Program (PROAGRI), each of the public agricultural services prepared master plans for the 1999–2004 period. In the conceptualization phase of the preparation of the plans, there was a crosschecking of principal activities with emphasis on the complementary components such as research, extension and support to agricultural production. The principal objective of this exercise was to avoid duplication of functions and ensure that each component was within its institutional scope. However, there was a lack of depth in the analysis of horizontal institutional linkages and the relationship among the budget, financing, and annual M&E of each of the eight components of PROAGRI. To date, both research and extension plan and budget their activities in isolation.

Crop research and extension normally interact during the implementation of common interventions such as the diffusion of the Vitamin A–enriched sweet potatoes and improved production and processing of cassava (Nampula and Inhambane provinces). The conception and prioritizing of "on station" research is a topic that is rarely discussed jointly with extensionists. In 2002 one of the four agronomic stations in the country (Lichinga) had a formal working collaboration with extension that included on-farm research on problems of farmers in surrounding extension networks. The Nampula agronomic research post was currently working with extension on identifying cassava varieties that are resistant to brown streak disease. In livestock research, the Ulóngue research station in the highlands of Angónia, had a formal partnership with extension to carry out research on feed management and cattle breeding. An excellent example of collaboration between veterinary research and extension is the joint research and extension program on Newcastle disease in chickens. Extension performed an important job in on farm testing of the first Mozambican vaccine. But most successful research and extension linkages are based on personal relationships between researchers and extension managers and with a constant turnover of staff—both extension and research—it is hard to develop trust and joint activities.

There are some important institutional constraints on increasing research and extension connectivity. First, salaries are relatively low in the public sector (US$400 per month for B.Sc. and about US$600 per month for M.Sc.) and about US$900 for the Ph.D.[2] As a result, there is a high turnover of extension and research staff. Second, there is a lack of non-monetary incentives (housing, office space and transport) to attract capable and experienced researchers and extensionists to relocate to the field. Third, there is a lack of transparent and credible professional career paths and incentive packages to attract extension specialists and researchers to spend a substantial block of time (five to ten years) in the field. For example, an extensionists or a subject matter specialist with ten years of work experience receives the same salary as a new technician just starting work. The same is true for the technicians working for research. But the December 2004 reorganization of research into a single institute with both thematic and zonal centers, will help address some of these concerns and will enhance the connectivity between research and extension.

Without question, there is need for a socio-political assessment of the monetary and non-monetary incentives facing professionals in both the extension and research services. After seventeen years of public extension, it seems fair to pose the questions: why is there political and financial support to build houses for teachers and health workers in rural communities but not for agricultural extension staff? Even though there are no clear policy guidelines for the provision of housing, some provincial Directorates of Agriculture are building houses based on decisions made at the provincial level. Also, what is the number of qualified researchers and extensionists that are needed to form a "critical mass" of researchers and extensionists capable of building a strong national agricultural science base and technology delivery system? The questions must be resolved if Mozambique is going to become competitive in regional and global markets.

Mozambique's INIA has four agricultural research stations (Umbeluzi, Chokwe, Sussundenga, and Lichinga) and three posts of agricultural research (Nampula, Namialo, and Nhacoongo) (Bias and Donovan 2003). There are three livestock research stations (Ulongue, Chobela, and Mazimchopes). One livestock research station is located in the south in low altitude areas (20–200m) and the other in the east central part of the country (800–1,000 m). There are two forestry experiment centers (Marracuene and Sussundenga). One forestry research center (CEF) is located in the lowlands and the other in the highlands of the country. In general, the forestry research centers are active, especially in multiplying eucalyptus and pine seedlings and carrying out studies of the sustainable use of natural resources. But table 4 reveals that the number of scientists within the research system of Mozambique is extremely low for a nation of 19 million and the level of education of the scientists is low for a national agricultural research system in the twenty-first century. For example Botswana has 101 full-time equivalent researchers and it has only 1.7 million people (Beintema et al. 2004).

To summarize, Mozambique has a vast array of agro-ecological regions and 34 million hectares of arable land. On-farm research is urgently needed to develop location specific technology for Mozambique's 3.3 million small-scale farms. However, because of budget constraints on INIA and public extension, some NGOs (SG 2000) and SARRNET (Southern Africa Root Crop Research Network) have been requested to finance on-farm trials, and co-finance demonstrations of new agro-processing technologies, in partnership with research and agricultural equipment suppliers. These on-farm trials have led to the release of a quality protein maize variety (Sussuma) in 2001 and some maize hybrids developed in Zimbabwe and South Africa by private seed companies.

Soil conservation and conservation tillage are important areas of extension and research collaboration because of soil degradation in the highlands such as Lichinga and Sanga (Niassa Province); Manica, Sus-

**Table 4.** Technical Staff of Research Institutions, 2004

| INSTITUTION | LEVEL OF EDUCATION | | |
|---|---|---|---|
| | Ph.D. | M.Sc. | B.Sc. |
| INIA | 8 | 15 | 22 |
| INIVE | 1 | 10 | 9 |
| IPA | 1* | 6** | 10 |

*Currently studying  **Two staff currently studying

sundenga, Mussurize, and Gondola (Manica province); Angónia and Tsangano (Tete province); and Gorongosa (Sofala province). These are the major maize and bean production zones of the country where research on soil fertility and conservation is of paramount importance. Over the last five years, extension has helped develop minimum and zero tillage technologies through 0.5 ha demonstration plots (Nhancale 2000). On the other hand, in Manica and Sofala provinces, about 500 plots of 0.5 ha were established by planting vetiver grass and placing stones along contour lines to reduce erosion. Research is urgently needed on the economics of soil conservation and conservation tillage because the latter requires the application of herbicides which are expensive and require farmer knowledge about the timing and frequency of chemical use. In summary, in spite of some progress, research and extension linkages remain weak.

### NGO Extension Activities

In 2004 there were seventy-one (thirty-nine national and thirty-two international) NGOs providing extension services in Mozambique. Appendix 2 shows the provincial coverage of national and international NGOs and private firms hiring extension workers. The introduction and spread of NGO extension has spurred the following changes in extension in Mozambique:

- *Increase in geographical coverage:* Various rural areas that were previously without extension are now served by NGO extension services. However, there were no criteria to guide the establishment of NGOs throughout the country. As a result, there is a heavy concentration of extension in some provinces and duplication of public and NGO extension in a few districts.

- *Accelerated technology transfer:* The relatively large budgets of the international NGOs accelerated the transfer of technology and linkages with regional and international research institutions (ICRAF, Malawi; IITA, Nigeria) and regional seed companies.

- *Serving remote districts:* Some of the NGOs in remote districts with low agricultural potential performed an important social role in assisting subsistence farmers and remote communities.

- *Human Capital Improvement:* The NGOs used their flexibility and financial capacity to hire a large number of B.Sc. and M.Sc. graduates on fixed term contracts (typically two years) and posted them at provincial and district levels. However, the common problem in phasing out donor-financed NGO projects is that the local technical staff members move on to new jobs and carry with them their local knowledge of the technical, economic and social factors that are important in agricultural development.

- *Increased competition and cooperation:* The entrée of NGOs into the extension arena has introduced a note of healthy competition between the three main extension providers. On the one hand, the entrée of NGOs increased the number of extension models, thus opening the door to learning by doing and learning from each other. However, from 1993 to 1997, with the exception of three cases, there were no formal cooperative agreements between public and NGOs extension.[3] During this period agricultural district authorities received little information about NGO extension programs or projects. The three extension providers should be encouraged to exchange annual work plans, financial reports and convene semi-annual meetings.

Over the past six years, a number of NGOs have consolidated, terminated, or reoriented their programs. Many of these changes were motivated by changes in donor policies and available funding rather than by decisions of the government or local communities where NGOs were operating. Nevertheless, a number of new and ambitious NGO extension programs were launched because many donors favored financing extension through the NGOs, especially international NGOs. The NGOs in Mozambique have relatively large budgets for agricultural programs. For example, World Vision's annual budget for agricultural projects in Mozambique was around US$5 million in 2004. The total European Union investment in Mozambique for extension programs, nutrition and food security was around 31 million from 2000 to 2003. Today the Provincial Agricultural Extension office requires all NGOs in the province to keep the provincial offices informed of their work plans.

According to Ye et al. (2003) the majority of NGOs working in agriculture in Mozambique are working on specialized issues such as food production, gender and environment, leadership and management, advocacy and lobbying, agro business and marketing, farmers organization, and HIV/AIDS. However, the few available global studies of the economics of extension show that the cost of extension per producer per year is highly variable and that most of them do not include the benefits—direct and indirect—of the interventions. Likewise, there is little empirical information on cost recovery, i.e. the portion of the total cost of extension that is paid by individual farmers or commodity associations. The best evidence on cost recovery in the developing world is found in Chile where, after twenty-five years of experimentation with the private delivery of extension services, the government was still financing about 85 percent of the total cost of extension and the farmers were only paying 15 percent in 2000 (Berdegue and Marchant 2002).

## Building New Partnerships

Building new partnerships and linkages with regional and global research networks is a priority of public extension (Swanson 2004). These partnerships should also include public, NGO, and private sector linkages; agricultural input and equipment suppliers; commodity organizations;

agricultural unions; and agricultural training institutions (Gemo and Rivera 2001).

The supply of certified seed in Mozambique is dominated by the SEED CO based in Zimbabwe and PANNAR based in South Africa. SEED CO was formed by a merger of the SEED co-op of Zimbabwe and "Sementes de Moçambique" (SEMOC, Lda) in 2000. PANAR entered the seed market in Mozambique in 2000. From the mid-1980s to the 1990s, SEMOC channeled about 90 percent of its total seed stock to humanitarian agencies for free distribution to farmers affected by natural calamities and the war. For example, from 1989 to 1996, SEMOC distributed 72,463 tons of seeds through emergency channels.

The emergency was officially terminated in 1996 but Mozambique continued to experience natural calamities such as the big floods of 2000 and 2001 and drought in some regions of the south and central regions in 2001–2. Following these calamities, the free or subsidized distribution of certified seed and/or grain benefited thousands of farmers. Although, the free distribution or highly subsidized sale of seed is understandable in emergency conditions, it has created the following constraints on building seed markets:

- *Market distortion:* lethargy in the development of seed market in general and a lack of interest of seed companies in penetrating the retail seed market
- *Dependency of producers:* free seed promoted a dependency mentality and opportunism by producers in pressing for free or subsidized seed
- *Negative influence in the dissemination and adoption of technologies:* free seed distribution was a constraint on the development of a culture of farmers buying seed

On the other hand, the lack of a clear national policy on managing international food assistance has affected farm incentives. For example, grain has frequently been imported for the main consumption centers at harvest time, thus depressing domestic grain prices. One rationale for food aid is the high transaction costs of moving grain from the north and central regions to consumption zones in the south. There is some evidence that there are distortions in input markets—especially seed. Since 1998 seed companies have started to penetrate rural areas where the public extension service had collaborated with the seed companies in installing thousands of demonstration plots (1,000 m²) throughout the country, especially along rural roads. Today some seed companies cater to emergency relief markets and the Ministry of Agriculture has shifted from the free distribution of seed to organizing seed fairs.

Public extension has also worked closely with distributors of inorganic fertilizers, herbicides, insecticides and fungicides and helped develop and diffuse packages to promote the intensive and semi-intensive cultivation of maize, rice, sunflower, and groundnuts. Apart from these demonstrations, partnerships have been developed among the suppliers of inputs, public extension (also private), and rural merchants and/or NGOs that are promoting the establishment of farmer organizations. Within the scope of this partnership, farmers receive inputs on credit, the extension service provides technical assistance and the merchants and/or NGOs help find a market for the produce. However, low output prices and high transport costs are hampering this type of initiative.

However, public extension has collaborated with suppliers of agricultural equipment by organizing demonstrations of small-scale processing equipment for the family sector. In 2000, public extension collaborated with two large national enterprises (AGRO-ALFA and KANES) in the training of technicians and the manufacturer of cassava processing machines. A prototype machine from the International Institute of Tropical Agriculture (IITA) Ibadan, Nigeria, reduced the labor necessary for processing one ton of cassava by one fourth and also reduced the cyanide acid of cassava to a tolerable level. In 2000 and 2003, public extension and manufacturing enterprises carried out sixty public demonstrations of cassava processing machines in high potential rural areas. The costs of manufacturing these machines and demonstration of their use were co-financed by extension and SG 2000. However the lack of credit schemes in rural zones constitutes a constraint on the acquisition of the machines by farmers and farmer associations. In 2003, only ten machines with a processing capacity of eight tons per day were operating in rural areas of Nampula and Inhambane provinces.

From 1998 to 2003, some progress was achieved in strengthening linkages between public and NGO extension providers (Gemo 2000). One example is the mutually beneficial partnership between public extension and CLUSA, an American NGO working in Nampula province. Public extension provided technical advice to farmers and extensionists and supervisors developed a plan of work that was approved, monitored and evaluated jointly by public extension and CLUSA. CLUSA has the responsibility of promoting the formation of farmer organizations and carrying out leadership training programs. CLUSA also facilitated access to input markets (especially improved seeds) as well as linkages with product markets (Clusa 2001). The DNER/CLUSA partnership produced satisfactory results during three consecutive agricultural seasons, but the partnership started to weaken because of the instability in maize prices starting from 1999, especially in the northern region of the country. The DNER partnership with CLUSA revealed that CLUSA had more efficient logistical support for its staff and it paid substantially higher salaries than the public sector.

Swanson and Samy (2002) look ahead and describe the opportunities for new extension partnerships:

> The role of public sector extension will continue to evolve during the twenty-first century as new organizations take their place in rural communities and compete with public extension for time and resources. Public extension should not view these new organizations as threats, but as opportunities to forge new partnerships. However, for these new partnerships to develop, policymakers must create a positive policy environment that will specify an appropriate division of labor between public extension, private agribusiness firms, and NGOs.

## Outsourcing Extension

Outsourcing extension is currently a lively topic because many donors have praised outsourcing approaches such as gradual privatization (in the

Netherlands), partial cost recovery (in England), and commodity extension programs (Dairy Board) in New Zealand (Van den Ban and Hawkins
1996; Rivera and Carey 1997).[4] The DNER manual defines outsourcing as
"the act of public sector extension of involving the private sector (whether
private companies, NGOs, farmer associations, or registered individual
extension consultants) to assume responsibility for providing extension
services, in part or in full" (DNER 2001). Gemo and Rivera (2002) report
that the pillars of the Extension Master Plan are: institutional pluralism
of extension providers, integrated National Extension System (SISNE)
and multiple financial and delivery arrangements.[5] DNER has adopted
learning by doing philosophy to find answers to three questions:

- How to nurture and develop an array of public and private extension
  providers?
- How to empower farmers and farmer organizations to enable them
  to inject strong doses of local knowledge into priority setting and the
  voice of farmers in the hiring and firing of local extension workers?
- How can extension be financed over time?

The utilization of external funds, channeled through the public extension services to finance the contracting of services to a third party such
as consulting companies, local and international NGOs, farmer associations, and commodity groups, was promoted by the World Bank and
endorsed by the Ministry of Agriculture. Outsourcing was first launched
in 1993 as part of the first World Bank project to rehabilitate public extension in Mozambique—the Agricultural Services Rehabilitation and Development Project (World Bank 2001). In 1993, the Joint Venture Companies
(JVC) for cotton production were asked to prepare proposals to provide
private extension services to smallholders in the provinces of Nampula
and Cabo-Delgado. The selected JVC, included Portuguese, Mozambican,
and Lonrho capital, and it coordinated cotton production by smallholders under contract. However, when cotton was cultivated by smallholders
in parcels of 0.5 to 1.0 hectares, it usually did not generate enough revenue to ensure the food security of smallholders. Therefore, the JVC was

asked to provide extension assistance on maize in order that the cotton-producing smallholders could grow enough maize to meet their family food security needs. But the JVC's proposed budget to supply private extension assistance to smallholders turned out to be very expensive. In fact, in some cases, it included charges for heavy equipment and transport as well as the cost of inputs on credit for cotton producers. Therefore, the government abandoned the idea of contracting (outsourcing) agricultural services in 1994; but it was renewed in 1996, when two districts in Cabo-Delgado were handed over to Lonrho, Mozambique. But the JVCs in Cabo-Delgado were plagued with unforeseen legal and administrative problems surrounding the transfer of goods (especially houses, vehicles, and motorcycles) and financial issues.

■ Two Types of Outsourcing

There are two options for outsourcing extension. The first is for donors to contract directly with international NGOs to deliver extension assistance to smallholders. The second is for the government to outsource extension. The first option is the most common type of outsourcing extension in Mozambique; it includes almost all of the donors that finance extension activities with the exception of the World Bank and IFAD. Some international NGOs have recently developed partnerships with national NGOs in Mozambique, but national NGOs often find it difficult to obtain a reliable source of revenue generation to ensure their sustainability and continuity.

Three instruments are used by NGOs to develop outsourcing plans with donors: programs and/or projects, annual plans of activities, and budgets. M&E reports are important in monitoring the performance of the relationship between the contractor and the NGOs. However, most of the external evaluators are selected by the NGOs; but in some cases, donors are involved in the selection of evaluators.

The degree of government involvement in the process of contracting NGOs by the donors depends on the openness of donors, leadership of the NGOs, and the time it takes to build trust and share financial statements, etc. For example: USAID, one of the major financiers of international

NGOs since the early 1990s, waited until 2001 to invite the Ministry of Agriculture to comment on its proposed financing of NGO extension programs. In the second option, the government institutions and/or public services are active parties in contracting, control, and evaluation of the provision of extension services by the third party.

The public extension service performs three roles in promoting outsourcing in Mozambique. First, it searches for funds to finance medium and long-term (five to ten years) public extension programs. These are made operational according to the annual plan of activities and budget (PAAOs) that are discussed and approved in annual sessions between the Ministry of Agriculture and donor representatives. Part of the PAAO funds of public extension are used to finance the contracting of extension services to non-governmental entities. The second role of public extension is to maintain an effective M&E system, a major challenge to a relatively new public extension service. A rigorous M&E verification of public expenditures is needed to compare the quality and range of services and the economics of public, private, and non-governmental extension services. The third role is to promote the involvement of national NGOs and private firms in outsourcing extension, a task that is difficult in a country dominated by international NGOs. This role is relatively complex, but it is a necessary process for developing extension models that are technically sound and economically sustainable.

### ■ Implementation of Outsourcing

In Mozambique, outsourcing has been pursued on an ad hoc basis for more than a decade through what has been called a "patchwork of donor-funded projects." During the second phase of extension from 1993 to 1997, numerous international and local NGOs provided extension services to farmers (Crowder and Anderson 2001, 113). During the mid-1990s, private JVCs were partially reimbursed for providing extension services to the family sector (World Bank 2001).[6] A JVC working in a cotton zone was selected by DNER to deliver extension services to the family sector but the JVC's financial terms were unacceptable and the program failed. Crowder and Anderson reports that the chosen JVC "felt entitled to incentives or subsidies from the government" which were "60 percent more costly" than the comparable public-sector extension services (2001, 116). A large number of NGOs (82) are currently delivering extension services to the family sector on contracts (outsourcing) financed by donors.

In Mozambique, there is growing recognition that crafting institutional reforms is a pragmatic, exploratory and social learning process that unfolds over years and decades. MADER/PROAGRI have endorsed a gradual and experimental approach to outsourcing (contracting out). DNER has developed a manual (DNER 2001) and terms of reference for outsourcing extension (DNER 2001a).

In October 2002, DNER selected a consortium of three NGOs and a private firm to carry out a three-year pilot study of outsourcing extension in Murrapula district in Nampula province. A private firm (working in association with one NGO) was chosen to carry out a similar study in Nicoadala district in Zambezia province. The total cost for the two outsourcing pilot programs is US$1.9 million dollars over the 2002–5 period. Similar three-year pilot programs were planned to be initiated in Niassa and Gaza provinces in 2003, but they have been put on hold because of budget ceiling problems. The coordination unit of outsourcing within DNER,[7] summarized the implementation status of outsourcing in Murrupula and Nicoadala in August 2004 as follows:

- Communication is constructive among the providers with DNER, provincial, and district offices of agriculture as well as with other partners, but it needs to be improved.
- The monitoring and supervision by the district office of agriculture needs to be strengthened in such a manner as to ensure the integrity of the outsourcing process.
- The exchange of experience with other outsourcing initiatives in Mozambique is weak.
- The service providers are accomplishing some work, but it is too early to arrive at estimates of the economics of outsourcing and its financial sustainability and possible replication.

In 2002, the EU in collaboration with the Mozambican institutes of cashew and cotton signed a contract with two NGOs for the provision of extension and food security services with emphasis on cotton and cashew crops valued at $11 million for a period of five years. Naturally, outsourcing raises many questions. Outsourcing has a high initial cost but costs represent only one side of the cost-benefit equation. Information is urgently needed on the benefits, i.e. the impact of outsourced extension on farmers and rural communities. The benefits of the DNER outsourcing experiment are unclear at this early stage of implementation but after two or three years, we should be able to answer the question of whether farmers in the outsourcing districts of Nampula and Zambezia provinces achieved higher yields and incomes than farmers served by DNER extensionists in the same province. Currently public extension has an annual budget of US$32,000 to $40,000 per district served, but the cost of the outsourced extension in the study districts will be an average of US$200,000 per district per year. These questions are going to be answered with a carefully designed baseline survey, periodic evaluations, and through a careful documentation of the entire outsourcing experiment.

■ Outsourcing: Can Poor Farmers Buy Their Way Out of Poverty?

Three lessons emerge from global outsourcing experiments:

❶ The first lesson is that building an array of private and NGO extension service providers is a complex and arduous task. The stage of a nation's institutional development and the degree of farmer participation in the market economy are critical factors in determining the scope for building and financing a competitive group of extension service providers. In Chile free vouchers were offered to farmers in 1978 to use in purchasing extension assistance; but after six years of corruption and market failure (i.e. a lack of private extension providers to compete with each other in rural areas), vouchers were abandoned (Berdegue and Marchant 2002). Although the academic literature is limited on this topic, CLUSA's experience in building "income generating" farmer support groups in a restricted area is promising and it should be carefully studied by DNER (CLUSA 2001).

❷ The second lesson is that international NGOs represent a proven model to deliver extension services. Some of this success is attributed to a generous flow of foreign aid, hiring the best local and foreign people, and working in circumscribed project areas. They have helped test and transfer best practices and shown how to develop incentives to recruit, promote, and retain Mozambican managers and extension workers. However, the international NGOs that depend on foreign aid for the bulk of their financing are unlikely to be financially sustainable over the long run. In our opinion, the Ministry of Agriculture should request donors to agree to gradually shift their financial support from international to local NGOs and increase their support to DNER over a 10–15–year transition period, as international NGOs are withdrawing.

❸ Third, it has been easier to develop a pluralistic system of extension providers than to reduce the total public expenditure on extension. Even in a middle-income country such as Chile, the public expenditure on extension still represents 85 to 90 percent of the total extension budget after twenty-two years (1978–2000) of nurturing private and NGO extension providers. To summarize, the Ministry of Agriculture and the Minister of Finance should assume that even if an array of NGO and private extension service providers emerge over time, the government of Mozambique will most likely be the main financier of extension for decades to come.

In our judgment, outsourcing is premature in many African countries with limited market participation of farmers, weak institutions, poor roads, and limited private sector involvement in input delivery and marketing. The experience to date suggests that Mozambique has made a wise decision to adopt a "gradual approach" (PROAGRI 2000) to outsourcing. Without question, the outsourcing experiments now underway by the DNER and the European Commission in Mozambique and public funding of privately delivered extension services in Uganda are valuable learning-by-doing exercises (Nahdy et al. 2002).[8]

## Cost Recovery

Campbell and Barker (1997) contend that the viability of public extension recommendations should be analyzed from two perspectives. The first is the ability of farmers to manage and produce a crop within their own environment. The second is the results (profitability) that can be achieved by them. The authors argue that the technical viability can be observed in a holistic environment on the farmers' fields. The yield variability on the initial DNER/SG 2000 demonstration plots was initially high; but in 1996–97, some farmers got 5.5 tons of maize per hectare and 5 tons of rice, although many farmers using the same technological package got 2.0 to 2.5 tons in the same period and in subsequent agricultural seasons. The results demonstrated that there was a good biological response to the package, but the bottom line is whether the package is profitable—not just whether yields can be doubled or tripled. The easy task is to measure yields and tally up the cost of production. For example, the certified open-pollinated maize seeds cost 10 to 12 times more than the price of the grain, while the hybrids cost 12 to 15 times more in rural areas. Currently, one ton of inorganic fertilizer costs about US$300 to $350 at the farm level. Nhancale (2000) found that maize was profitable when farmers produce a minimum of 4 tons per hectare. The challenge is to identify recommendation domains where the package is profitable and constraints on production are removed, such as fragmented input markets and low grain prices at harvest time. These factors constrain the intensification of food crop production.

Cost recovery is an appealing concept in theory, but in practice has been difficult to get poor farmers in poor countries to pay for extension services. Why? First it is difficult to finance extension services in subsistence and semi-subsistence economies that do not have agricultural exports to tax. The decentralization of extension to the district level raises taxable capacity by enabling farmers "to see what they are getting for their taxes" (Lewis 1967). If local extension workers help farmers generate new income streams (e.g., sesame and paprika) that can be taxed as exports, some of the tax revenue can be used by local governments to cost-share extension. Also, the higher incomes accruing to paprika farmers, for example, can enable a producer association of paprika or sunflower growers to pay for part or all of the costs of extension services. The second reason why it is difficult for poor farmers in Africa to pay part or all of the cost of extension is explained by the low degree of commercialization of agriculture in Africa as compared to Asia. In China, for example, 80 to 90 percent of the farmers purchase fertilizer compared with 3 percent in Mozambique, one of the lowest percentages in Africa. To summarize, in subsistence and semi-subsistence economies in Africa, there is limited income for farmers to "buy their way out of poverty," i.e. by paying directly or indirectly for extension assistance.

### ■ Promoting Diversification and High-Value Crops

Starting with the 1997–98 agricultural season, NGOs have made a special point of promoting high-value crops such as paprika, sesame, sunflower, pulses, and soya, which are capable of producing new income streams for poor farmers. The promotion of these crops normally relies on partnership among NGOs, agricultural input suppliers, and farmers, and they have the most potential in the high-altitude areas in the north and center of the country. In most seasons, farmers have had problems securing access to quality seed. The seed supply is still limited, but a seed market is emerging. The training of extensionists about high-value crops is a new challenge as most of them do not have the technical knowledge required for production of these crops; how to add value to the commodities and how to find information about prices, grades, and standards; WTO regulations; and access to regional and global markets. For example, in 2001 in Nampula province, farmers harvested 3,000 tons of sesame; but because of poor quality, the prospective buyer reduced the pre-established price, and the export contract was not consummated. The production of sunflower in Manica province reached 2,000 tons in 2001, an increase of 300 percent in five years. However, the oil extraction rate of sunflower in Manica is 40 percent compared to 60 percent in South Africa and Zimbabwe. But the national research system has given priority to basic food crops. As a result, there is limited technical information on high-value crops for small-scale farms in Mozambique. Since some of the high-value crops are being promoted throughout Southern Africa, it will be important to obtain information on prices, markets, and profitability. In this regard the market information provided by SIMA is especially valuable.

## ■ The Decline of Private Extension: 1999–2004

Two factors have constrained the performance of private extension from 1999 to 2004. The first relates to the government's use of the concession model to allocate large blocks of land to private companies and the JVCs. As mentioned, soon after the end of Civil War, the government and the private sector formed a number of JVCs to rehabilitate the cotton sector. The second has been the decline in the international prices of cotton fiber. The consequences of these two factors have undermined the growth of private companies and the income of thousands of farmers who signed a cotton contract. During the mid-1990s the keen competition between concessionaires and non-concessionaires raised the price of cotton to farmers and forced the Ministry of Agriculture to intervene in order to resolve the dispute between the new cotton enterprises and old concessionaires. In 1998, the government approved a strategy of gradually liberalizing the concession system and allowing the non-concessionaires to operate within the perimeter of the concessionaires, but in a coordinated manner. The dispute and increased competition challenged the profitability and the future of the concessionaires. The higher prices offered by non-concessionaires encouraged producers to sell their cotton to the new companies. Since the new companies did not have a large investment in technical assistance and agricultural inputs on credit, most of them were able to offer higher prices to smallholders than those of the concessionaires. The dispute between the concessionaires and non-concessionaires over the purchase price of cotton was followed by a plea from the industry for subsidies. Although this benefited the farmers in the short run, it was subsequently harmful to most farmers. Over the 1998–2002 period, cotton prices fell to their lowest level in thirty years (Boughton et al. 2002). In Mozambique, the average price of export FOB, first-grade, cotton fiber was reduced by about 60 percent, from US$1,400 in 1995 to $600 in 2002. This dramatic reduction had obviously affected the financial sustainability of the entire cotton supply chain.

Over the last decade, however, tobacco production has increased from roughly 3,000 tons in 1997–98 to 37,000 tons in 2002–3. A significant part of the tobacco crop is for export markets. Currently, tobacco production is being encouraged in the Angonia and Tsangano highland and in other districts of Tete and Niassa. Some cotton concessionaires are promoting the production of tobacco on a limited scale in Nampula, Cabo-Delgado, and Niassa provinces. In Manica province, there are several private farmers and companies involved in the production of tobacco. The pattern of production is similar to that of cotton. The companies sub-contract with farmers and provide seed and fertilizer on credit that is deducted during the sale of produce to the companies.

From 1990 to 1999, the government's KR II program imported agrochemicals and agricultural equipment from Japan that was almost exclusively used by the private sector and the cotton concessionaires. The KR II program was financed by the government of Japan's foreign aid contribution to Mozambique. The sugar estates and cotton concessionaires received agro-chemicals and equipment on credit at roughly two-thirds of international prices. But delays in the importation of these goods resulted in logistical problems and the limited competition often elevated prices above international levels. The implementation of this program was criticized because it undermined the development of the agro-chemical market. In part because of these difficulties, the program was terminated in 1999.

### NOTES

1. These provinces used to request the National Directorate of Rural Extension to release funds on a quarterly basis. The requests were then referred to the World Bank and IFAD (for endorsement), the two main financiers of public extension. The central level used to control the budget ceiling of the provincial services in accordance with the availability of counterpart government funds (5 to 10 percent).

2. Based on February 2005 official exchange rate of US$1 = Mts 18,500.

3. There were three exceptions. IBIS (Danish) and Molisv (Italian) collaborated with public

extension respectively in Zambezia and Gaza provinces and SG 2000 drew on public extension staff to implement some extension activities.

4. NGOs have outsourced extension with donor aid for more than a decade. DNER and the EU launched outsourcing in 2002.

5. For case studies on outsourcing extension see (Rivera and Zijp 2002; Crowder and Anderson 2001).

6. State-owned cotton companies were partially privatized in the late 1980s by the formation of Joint Venture Companies (JVCs) through investments by international agribusinesses (Crowder and Anderson 2001).

7. Ponto de Situacao Sobre o Outsourcing no MADER, August 2004

8. Michael Abu Foster of the Sasakawa Program in Uganda reports that in 2000 Uganda launched a new program of public funding of privately delivered extension advisory services through the National Agricultural Advisory Services (NAADS). However, the program is now five years old and it is running into some problems. These include concerns about the quality of advisory services provided by private firms, the lack of continuity in awarding contracts to private firms, frequent changes of service providers, and long breaks between contracts (Sasakawa African Association 2005).

# CHAPTER 6

# Appraisal of the Implementation of the First Extension Master Plan: 1999–2004

The goal of the first Extension Master Plan was to develop a pluralistic national system of public, NGO, and private extension providers guided by increasing demand pressure from empowered farmers and producer organizations. The Plan stated that the public sector will require a "minimum core competency" of 300 public extension workers (as civil servants) out of a total of 696 extentionists and 84 field supervisors for a period of five years to disseminate "public good" technology to the family sector, develop human resource for the overall system, and coordinate and disseminate successful experiences among extension providers. The Plan was endorsed and incorporated into the PROAGRI Program of work for the 1999–2004 period.[1] The Extension Master Plan identified three factors limiting agricultural development that required attention:

- Weakness in technical messages
- Insufficient training of extension workers

- Inadequate management, including weaknesses in implementation, supervision and financial disbursements in MADER

The first Extension Master Plan asserted that "there is a backlog of technological options and experience (either from other farmers, the research system, or extension activities in the other parts of the country) that can be taken advantage of" (DNER 1997, 12–13). But the Plan undermines this optimistic assessment by contending that there is a "weakness in technical messages," which seems to imply that the technology is not profitable to family farms. However, numerous studies decry the lack of profitable technology on the shelf for the family sector (Danida 2002, 2002a; DNER 2002). A field visit to six districts in 2002 revealed that there was a lack of micro economic studies of present and improved technology for the family sector and a general lack of connectivity between research stations and posts (research) and extension programs. For example, three of the four main research stations visited were inactive in mid-2002 because of disbursement delays, lack of qualified staff, and inadequate computer and support services (Eicher 2002). The bottom line is that Mozambique's agricultural research system has been hampered by uncertainties about the organizational structure of research and burdened by a shortage of staff and operating funds and delays in developing the new zonal research centers. The Institute of Agrarian Research in Mozambique (IIAM) was created in late 2004 and is now addressing these issues. IIAM plans to add socio-economic research capacity to assist extension providers by measuring the impact of their recommended technologies and crop management practices.

The first Extension Master Plan flagged insufficient training of extension workers as a major problem because 76 percent of the 700 public extension agents in 1996 had less than the minimum level of education (thirteen years of formal schooling). And today in 2005, the "quality" of human capital of front-line extension workers is still low, because it has proven difficult to garner donor funds to train and elevate the large number of front-line extension workers with a certificate. Appendix 1 shows that at the end of 2004 a total of 226 DNER extension workers had a certificate degree, even though the target of the First Extension Plan (1999 to 2004) was for all DNER workers to have a diploma or above by 2004.

The third factor affecting the performance of extension is the financing and management of the national extension system over time. Unfortunately, the debate on financing agricultural extension and research services in Africa has been sterile for the past decade because it usually starts by pre-selecting a target number of extensionists or researchers that would be desirable and then trys to figure out how such a target can be financed through levies, competitive grant schemes, and others. The more relevant questions are: what is the size of the extension system that can be economically justified to accelerate technology transfer and agricultural growth over time and what size can be financed by domestic resources, cost recovery and external (public and private) funds over time?[2]

Turning to the size question, the first Extension Master Plan introduced a vague concept called "minimum core competency" of public extension and then set an arbitrary ceiling of about 800 public extensionists with only 300 of the 800 employed on civil service terms and the balance on annual contracts. The Plan asserted that 800 would represent "a satisfactory number of extensionists and supervisors at the district level with specific training and professional experience in extension" (DNER 1997, 12). However, the Extension Master Plan reports that "insufficient training" was one of the three principal factors limiting the performance of DNER (DNER 1997, 3).

The first Extension Master Plan (DNER 1997) assumed that each public extension worker would assist 225 farm families directly and about 775 farm families indirectly or roughly 1,000 families per extension worker. Therefore, it is assumed that the 700 public extension workers would reach roughly 700,000 farm families or about 25 percent of the 3 million farm families in Mozambique.

We know of no developing country that has built a dynamic extension system with transient workers on one-year contracts, who gain a few years of experience in the public sector, then migrate to the NGOs and the private sector. The lack of transparent career advancement ladders is a source of frustration and poor professional attitude for front line extension workers, managers, and extension specialists. Until the Ministry of Agriculture develops a human resources strategy to solve some of these "incentive problems," DNER will continue to be undermined by high staff turnover and low-level professional development.[3]

The Master Plan discusses NGO extension providers and the gap in economic incentives between the public and NGO systems. The evidence shows that international NGOs have undermined the human capital base of DNER by offering salaries and benefits to extension workers that are at least double those offered by DNER. The lack of motorcycles and housing for front-line extension agents is also affecting the performance and morale of DNER extensionists.

The first Extension Master Plan endorsed pilot studies of outsourcing extension to non-governmental organizations such as NGOs and consulting firms. Several DNER staff spent much of year 2001 and part of 2002 preparing a manual and terms of reference for outsourcing studies (DNER 2001, 2001a). In October 2002, DNER launched a three-year pilot study of outsourcing in Nampula and Zambezia provinces. Even though several observers have criticized DNER for the delay in launching the outsourcing studies, it should be kept in mind that Chile rushed into outsourcing in 1978 and issued prepaid vouchers to enable farmers to purchase extension assistance from private providers. But Chile abandoned vouchers after six years because of hasty planning, corruption and market failure. Since learning by doing is an integral part of institution building, "one of the objectives of outsourcing is to help DNER develop the capacity to coordinate, oversee and regulate private sector providers (of extension) and to learn from the experiences of others" (Gemo and Rivera 2002, 151).

When the first Extension Master Plan was prepared, there was understandably little debate on global issues and the need for agriculture in developing countries to become regionally and globally competitive. The newly formed producer associations need access to market information to help farmers generate new income streams from value-added commodities through improved processing, marketing, and enhanced global competitiveness (Phillips and Serrano 1999). There is now an urgent need to develop a small cadre of research officers with knowledge and expertise in biotechnology and bio-safety, supply-chain management, trade, marketing, and agribusiness.[4] DNER should develop a close working relationship with the Department of Policy Analysis and draw on the pioneering research on agro-industrial development strategies (Benfica 2003) and the Agricultural Market Information System (SIMA) .

To summarize, the first Extension Master Plan (1999 to 2004) can be visualized as a valuable road map of experimental activities. However, many of these activities are under funded and constrained by system-wide and internal problems that should be addressed in the implementation of the 2005–9 Extension Master Plan. The future performance of DNER is critically dependent on correcting the incentive structure for extensionists, developing profitable technology and crop management practices for the family sector, and strengthening demand pressure from producer group and other stakeholders. But DNER cannot, by itself, solve system-wide problems such as the lack of incentives, job insecurity, and the limited connectivity between extension and research. Therefore, as DNER implements its second Master Plan for 2005–9, it will be important to discuss these "bread and butter" issues with the Human Resources Directorate, the Directorate of Economics, the Policy Analysis Department, IIAM, NGOs, and farm organizations and other clientele groups (Bias and Donovan 2003).

In early 2005 the number of extensionists employed by DNER and by NGOs (international and national) was approximately the same (table 5). Considerable thought should be given to the size, geographical coverage, and future expansion of DNER and NGOs during the second Extension Master Plan covering 2005–9 (DNER 2004).

Some important steps have been taken to improve the connectivity among extension, research, and farmers. The first annual research/extension conference in May 2003 helped set the tone for a sound partnership. We endorse the recent proposal by the Ministry of Agriculture to establish a "Unidade de Socioeconomia" within the new Institute of Agrarian Research of Mozambique (IIAM). The creation of IIAM and its four zonal

**Table 5.** Extensionists Employed by Public Extension and NGOs by Province, 2005

| PROVINCE | NUMBER OF EXTENSIONISTS | |
|---|---|---|
| | PUBLIC EXTENSION (DNER) | NGOS |
| MAPUTO | 46 | 46 |
| GAZA | 73 | 62 |
| INHAMBANE | 60 | 53 |
| SOFALA | 100 | 65 |
| MANICA | 83 | 52 |
| TETE | 53 | 18 |
| ZAMBEZIA | 63 | 167 |
| NAMPULA | 119 | 129 |
| NIASSA | 60 | 90 |
| CABO-DELGADO | 94 | 158 |
| *Subtotal* | *751* | *840* |
| DNER Central Staff | 19 | |
| *Grand Total* | *770* | *840* |

Source: DNER 2005

research stations is one of the main accomplishments of the on-going institutional reforms. The socio-economic unit will recruit and train agricultural economists and several extension specialists to carry out studies of farming systems, cost of production, diffusion, and acceptance and adoption of new technology with the aim of improving the technology development and diffusion system. The results of these field studies in different agro-ecological zones will provide a national database for accelerating the diffusion and spread of new technology and generating new income streams for the family sector. The impact studies produced by this new, socioeconomic research unit will be of great benefit to IIAM, DNER, NGOs, private extension, and external providers, as well as the donors financing PROAGRI.

## NOTES

1.  The Plan (DNER 1997) includes a number of valuable appendices about housing and transport issues for front-line extension workers that are germane to the implementation of the second Extension Master Plan for 2005–9.

2. In 2002 World Vision International, Maputo, reported that it employed 300 extension workers as follows: 200 extension technicians were in the field; 34 were extension specialists with a B.Sc. and above degrees and 62 were in support positions (Henderson 2002). There were 238 extension workers in Nampula province—a high-potential area— in 2002.

3. See Pavignani and Hauk (2002) and Sulemane and Kayizzi-Mugerwa (2003) for a discussion of incentives, reforms, and performance in the civil service of Mozambique.

4. See Berdegue, Reardon, and Escobar (2002); Weatherspoon and Reardon (2003); and Kherallah et al. (2002).

# CHAPTER 7

# Looking Ahead: Critical Issues for Policymakers, Extension Managers, and Donors

## The General Prescription and the Particular Case of Mozambique

Crafting Mozambican models of extension to meet the needs of small-scale farms is basically an accretionary (step-by-step) institution building process that unfolds slowly, pragmatically, and almost invisibly over time. What does it take to achieve this goal? The first step is to examine whether Mozambique should accept the advice of some donors to import models of extension from other continents. Other donors have urged downsizing public extension under the assumption that the private sector will expand its extension coverage and farmers will "cost share," i.e., pay part of the cost of extension. Without question, these general institutional prescriptions have been successful in some industrial countries, but they also have had a high rate of failure in developing countries at an early stage of institutional development. Nevertheless, the general prescription of importing global models of extension is appealing to many governments because it is often coupled with donor resources to pay for a new fleet of 4 x 4 vehicles and the cost of running the national extension system for a few years. But we must dig deeper and pose the question: What is in the best interests of the government and the people of Mozambique? General donor prescriptions or helping Mozambique craft extension models to address the particular case of Mozambique?

Starting in the 1980s, the proponents of structural adjustment programs exerted pressure on African governments to reduce public-sector employment and expenditures and move to a market economy. This general prescription has also been used to justify the reduction in the size and public expenditure on national research and extension services. In fact, Swanson (2004), recently reported that "with a few notable exceptions, donor support for extension systems in most developing countries came to a halt by the mid-1990s." But Africa is a complex continent of fifty-four countries at different stages of economic history and institutional development. As a result, it is unwise for donors to impose "general institutional prescriptions" for Africa.

Nevertheless, the T&V extension model was promoted by the World Bank as a general prescription for Africa starting in 1982 but it turned out to cost some 25–40 percent more than the systems it replaced (Anderson and Feder 2004). More recently, many academics and donor specialists have endorsed a new general prescription for extension that embraces decentralization, participation, outsourcing (contracting) and cost recovery with the goal of reducing the size of the government bureaucracy and public outlays on extension.[1] But despite the appeal of the general prescription of donors to downsize public extension systems throughout Africa, it does not follow that this general prescription should be adopted by Mozambique. Instead attention should be focused on building and crafting extension models for the particular case of Mozambique.

Mozambique is a particular case, a country at peace since 1992 and a country with one of the youngest and smallest public extension services in Africa. Moreover, Mozambique has a surprisingly small stock of human capital in both research and extension. Several comparisons of the stock of human capital add a sense of reality. In early 2005 Mozambique only had 1,838 extensionists[2] (public, private, and NGO) to serve its 3.3 million small-scale farms as compared with roughly 8,000 extensionists in Kenya and 6,000 in Zimbabwe. Moreover, the level of education of DNER technical staff is low.[3] We now turn to a discussion of three system-wide problems affecting the performance of extension in Mozambique, followed by a discussion of ten challenges facing extension in Mozambique over the coming five to ten years.

## System-Wide Problems

The Ministry of Agriculture and PROAGRI need to solve three system-wide problems that are constraining the performance of DNER: 1) discontinuity of donor support, 2) poor incentives for extensionists, and 3) a lack of profitable technology for extensionists to extend to farmers.

### ■ Discontinuity of Donor Support for PROAGRI

Extension is one of eight activities supported by PROAGRI. PROAGRI has now completed its first five years of operation; it has a number of accomplishments to its credit. First, PROAGRI has tightened financial accountability at central, provincial, and district levels. Field visits have revealed that the disbursement of funds has improved at the provincial level, but there are still some disbursement problems at the district level and at some research stations. Although it has taken time to improve financial disbursement, the (donor) partners supporting PROAGRI have praised this achievement. The second accomplishment is the decentralization of the Ministry of Agriculture. The third achievement is getting donors to exchange ideas and pool funds in exchange for one-stop accountability. Several field studies support these positive assessments. A World Bank mission to Sofala province reported in 2002: "In Sofala it is now generally established that PROAGRI resources are finally reaching the provinces and the public institutions of the agriculture sector are now comparatively better endowed to fulfill their tasks" (Sousa 2002). Two analysts recently concluded, "Even though much remains to be done, PROAGRI has successfully initiated a process of reform and modernization of Mozambican agriculture" (Garrido-Mirapeix and Toselli 2002).

However, in 2004 a number of donors raised questions about PRO-AGRI activities and delayed their annual financial contributions to

PROAGRI. The experience of PROAGRI over the 1999–2004 period has shown that the discontinuity of donor support can cripple PROAGRI and long-term, institution-building activities such as public extension and research (DNER 2004). For example, the erratic and delayed payment of donor aid to PROAGRI, especially in calendar year 2004, created a cash flow problem and curtailed the work of the DNER, disrupted long-term crop trials by researchers, and dampened the spirit of agricultural extension workers.

Given the long-term nature of building rural institutions, we recommend the government of Mozambique and donors stay the course and invest in PROAGRI and its components, including research and extension over the next two to three decades. The experience of Brazil, India, China, Malaysia, and more recently Viet Nam demonstrates that building an institutional foundation for a globally competitive agriculture cannot be achieved in a five- or ten-year time span.[4] Donors should be educated on the role that agriculture can play in the long run in improving the welfare of all mankind through the reduction of real (inflation adjusted) food prices over time. But the immediate problem for donors to address is their delayed contributions to PROAGRI. If donors terminate their support for PROAGRI after only five years of support, it will undercut the performance of DNER and the seven other programs being supported by PROAGRI. An authority on institution building captures the risk of changing the rules of donor support of an institutional innovation such as PROAGRI:

> One cannot, after setting off on an institution-building path, reverse directions or reorganize every few years. . . . Unilateral changing of the rules in the middle of the game of long-term institutional development breeds suspicion and conflict instead of cooperation and leads to a breakdown in the linkage between separately governed institutions. (Bonnen 1998, 284)

### ■ Incentives and Training for Knowledge Workers

The second system-wide problem impeding the work of DNER extensionists (knowledge workers) is the incentive problem—broadly defined to include monetary and non-monetary incentives and support facilities such as housing, transport, and training opportunities for career advancement. Nobel Laureate T.W. Schultz has shown that investments in human resources (formal, informal education, and on-the-job training) can make a significant contribution to economic development. The Ministry of Agriculture has developed a retrenchment strategy to reduce the number of employees of the Ministry, but human resource planning must go beyond retrenchment to address incentives, training, promotion, retention, career advancement, civil service status, housing, and means of transport—motorcycles or bicycles. Poor incentives are responsible for the high turnover of DNER staff in headquarters and in the field. For example, DNER has had three National Directors in the past eight years.

In meetings in six districts in May of 2002, front-line extension workers raised questions about incentives, housing, transport, and career advancement pathways for those on civil service terms and those on annual contracts (Eicher 2002). Contract extension workers were generally unaware that extensionists with a certificate or diploma over forty years of age could not be integrated into the civil service. The front-line agents were concerned about the public/NGO differential in salary, transportation, and housing, and reported that the NGO financial package was double or triple the value of that of DNER agents and researchers.[5] In Manica province, fifty-one of the DNER extensionists in 2002 were on annual contracts and only two were civil servants (Eicher 2002). Front-line extension workers feel as if they are second class clerks when compared to their counterparts in NGOs who enjoy substantially higher salaries and benefits.

Discussions with DNER extension workers revealed that they were also concerned about the need to travel long distances by bicycle from their homes to their assigned villages where they work with around three hundreds farmers. Several extension workers reported that they could increase the number of farmers served by 50 percent if they had a motorcycle, preferably on a "purchase and own" arrangement similar to the one developed by CLUSA (1999).[6] DNER should study the problem of motorcycle maintenance flagged in the DNER supervision mission to Gaza province (DNER 2002). The lack of government housing for extension workers was also a matter of concern. Although primary school teachers are given government housing near their school, the majority of extension workers have to find their own housing and ride bicycles 8 to 14 km to their assigned villages for work.

To summarize, the recruitment, training, incentives, promotion, and rewards for DNER staff at all levels are crucial issues that need to be debated and resolved. The incentive issues are constraining the ability of DNER to achieve its full potential. Without question, policy attention should focus on leveling the playing field between public and NGO extension workers.

### ■ Lack of Profitable Technology

The third cross-cutting issue affecting all three extension providers is the general lack of technology that is profitable to small-scale farms on a recurring basis and at an acceptable level of risk. Agricultural research in Mozambique has two fundamental roles to play in development. The first is to generate new technology to achieve family food security needs, farm profitability and natural resources goals. The second is to develop or import and adapt new technology to help farmers generate new income streams and rural employment from the sale of traditional and non-traditional commodities in local, regional, and global markets. The generation of new income streams from the production of high-value commodities such as paprika, turmeric, cardamom, cloves, annatto, and herbs (rosemary, basil, and sage) can raise taxable capacity on agricultural exports and help produce groups who eventually fund their own research on these crops.

The 1997 Extension Master Plan highlights the "lack of technology messages" as a key problem. But field visits to five research stations in mid-2002 reaffirmed the findings of a number of other studies showing that agricultural research is the weak link—perhaps the weakest link—in the agricultural knowledge triangle of research, extension, and higher agricultural education, in Mozambique (Eicher 2002 and PROAGRI 2002b). Field visits, interviews, and reports support the view that there is a lack of profitable technology for the family sector:

- A 2002 study concluded that the output of the four public research institutions in agriculture was "below expectations" (Royal Tropical Institute 2002, ii).

- Four of the five research stations visited in May 2002 were "inactive" (Eicher 2002). A few were facing financial disbursement problems. Only one social scientist was found in the visit to five research stations and posts. The visits revealed a heavy concentration on maize research. However, since the cost of fertilizer is US$350 to $400 a ton at the farm level, several NGOs reported at the time that they were not recommending the use of fertilizer on maize because it was not profitable. Many of the scientists in the research stations and posts appeared to be in limbo, awaiting guidance from Maputo on how the reform of the research system would affect their station/post and their careers.

- A study by agricultural economists of SG 2000 programs in Nampula and Manica provinces from 1996–97 to 1999–2000 revealed that the application of fertilizer increased smallholder maize yields, but due to the high cost of inputs and low maize prices, many farmers lost money (Howard et al. 1998, 2000, 2000a).

- An economic analysis of maize production in the northern part of Zambezia province found that "although there was a large biological response to fertilizer, the returns for using fertilizer were not particularly attractive due to the high cost of fertilizer, extra weeding needed on fertilized plots and the low price of maize" (Hilton and Xavier 1998/99).

- A DANIDA-sponsored study reported, "the research system remains largely unaffected by reform and maintains a top-down approach not geared toward responding to farmer needs or community requests" (DANIDA 2002). The report added that social scientists were urgently needed to relate technology development to on going policy reforms.

- A DNER supervision mission to Gaza province reported that there was "a shortage of available technological options"(DNER 2002).

- During a field visit in 2002, a provincial agricultural officer reported, "We need new technical messages. We have preached the same messages such as planting on line for ten years. We need messages on conservation farming, tobacco and other emerging crops, animal husbandry and fish farming" (Eicher 2002).

- The May 2001 meeting of PROAGRI concluded that it would take ten years to develop a productive research system (PROAGRI 2002). While this restructuring of research takes place, we recommend that social scientists in IIAM develop a list of best practices of technology and crop management practices for extension workers. For example, simple best-practice guidelines are needed for smallholder irrigation, conservation farming, and fertilized (micro dosing) application.


## Strengthening DNER: Ten Challenges

Ten challenges should be studied, debated ,and addressed in the course of implementing the second Extension Master Plan from 2005 to 2009.

❶ *Building Mozambican Models of Extension.* The institution-building challenge is to address the particular case of Mozambique and pragmatically craft a number of extension models based on pilot studies, local experience, and from other nations. The first Master Plan introduced the concept of a Unified Model of Extension (SUE) that calls for cooperation between DNER and Ministry of Agriculture Directorates of Animal Production and Forests and Wildlife. Field visits in 2002 revealed a number of promising partnerships between agriculture and livestock, but partnerships have proven to be more difficult to establish in forestry, partially because forestry extension agents have to enforce regulatory duties. Mozambique's two ongoing pilot studies of outsourcing extension are praiseworthy because they will provide insights based on conditions in Mozambique. The results of these outsourcing studies should be published and made available to extension experts throughout Africa. Likewise DNER should study the performance of the recently established Farmer Field School (FFS) model in several provinces in Mozambique and address three basic questions: do the field schools increase the knowledge of farmers? Has the increase in farmer knowledge led to higher crop yields and the adoption of new crop management practices? What is the cost of the FFS model as compared to the model that it is replacing?[7]

❷ *Redefining the Role of the Central Office of DNER, Provinces, and Districts.* The role of the DNER Directorate in Maputo should be redefined to provide overall vision, strategic direction, quality control, training, M&E, and mobilizing resources for the national extension system. The responsibility for implementing extension should shift to the provinces and districts in a progressive manner. The global experience reveals that the decentralization of research to the provincial/zonal level and the devolution of extension to the district level have paid rich dividends in many countries in terms of cost sharing and improved guidance on research priorities and feed back from farmers. Decentralization of extension to the district level and to rural communities can give "voice" to farmers and farm organizations. Much work remains to be done to empower extension management committees to make local extensionists more accountable. But caution should be exercised in charging extensionists with organizing farmer groups in situations where new technology is not available and access to markets is limited.

❸ *Geographical Coverage and Size of the National Extension System.* During the first Extension Master Plan (1999–2004), DNER increased its extension coverage from fifty-two to sixty-six districts. But DNER is under-funded to serve the present sixty-six districts. Since there is pressure on DNER to add even more districts over the 2005 to 2009 period, the global experience on this issue should be kept in mind. The global experience shows that there is a high payoff for concentrating extensionists in high-potential agro-ecologies and districts rather than sprinkling extensionists throughout the countryside. Therefore, priority should be given to strengthening DNER programs[8] in the sixty-six districts where DNER is currently functioning, and second priority should be given to adding DNER coverage in some new districts.

What has been learned about the size of national extension systems? In retrospect the decision of the first Extension Master Plan to set a ceiling of 800 public extension workers seems arbitrary and unwise (DNER 1997, 23). This decision was based on the assumption that the private sector and NGOs would expand their geographical coverage of extension. The Ministry of Agriculture should encourage DNER to develop guidelines for the geographical expansion and the size of DNER over the next five to ten years, including the districts where the DNER/NGO mix should be changed.[9]

❹ *Upgrading the Quality and Scope of Human Capital.* Africa's extension services have historically focused on agricultural production, not marketing and adding value to commodities (European Commission 1999; Coulter et al. 2004). In Mozambique, approximately 90 to 95 percent of all public extension workers are agricultural technicians and agronomists who are trained to help farmers increase crop and livestock production. However, the extension workers of the future must have the training, information, and resources to provide information on new technology, crop management practices, processing, marketing, health, and nutrition. The immediate human-capital challenge is to upgrade the quality of the staff in the DNER Central Office and front-line extension workers. Appendix 1 reveals that the current quality of DNER's front-line extension workers is low, partially because it has been difficult to get donors to support upgrading extension staff through short- and long-term training during the first five years of the Extension Master Plan. DNER should petition PROAGRI for more funds for short- and long-run training programs in the country and in the region.

The second human-capital issue is the need for DNER to add four or five subject-matter specialists in farm management, agro industry, processing, and marketing. The expertise of these specialists can help extension workers figure out how to help producer groups develop value-added commodity chains and search for new markets at home and in regional and global markets. To summarize, DNER needs to develop a Capacity-Building Strategic Plan to address both the problems of today and tomorrow.

❺ *The NGO Transition.* The international NGOs in Mozambique have proven to be reliable partners in humanitarian emergencies and, more recently, as productive partners in development. However, there are few examples of horizontal linkages and systematic exchange of substantive experience and financial information among Mozambique's three extension providers. Only a few of the larger international NGOs in Mozambique exchange annual reports with DNER. Only a few donors have invited DNER to critique the programs and annual plans of work of NGOs engaged in extension work. Presently, DNER does not have a voice in selecting the districts where new NGOs would like to launch extension programs. International NGOs represent a stopgap measure for meeting Mozambique's long-run human resource needs in the agricultural sector. Moreover, international NGOs can be self-perpetuating unless they are coupled with aggressive development of local technical and managerial capacities. Professor Gerald Helleiner of the University of Toronto recalls who benefited when the government of Tanzania relied heavily on expatriates for three decades:

A succession of expatriates learn more and more about developmental decision-making while the Africans below them in the hierarchy become progressively more alienated and discontented. The experience and collective "memory" which is accumulated during the process of development is thus appropriated by foreigners who subsequently leave the country carrying these invaluable assets with them. (Helleiner 1979)

The global experience reveals that after donor funding runs out, most international NGOs in agriculture and rural development are unable to mobilize enough private funds to self-finance and continue to implement extension and rural development programs. Therefore, it seems likely that many of the international NGOs in Mozambique are going to be financially unsustainable over the long pull. Therefore, we suggest that Ministry of Agriculture develop a strategy to guide the division of roles among the three main extension providers over the coming ten to twenty years.

❻ *Financing Extension.* There is growing evidence that privatization of the delivery of extension in most low-income countries has not been matched with cost recovery from farmers, lending further credence to the statement that "The poor cannot buy their way out of poverty" (by purchasing extension assistance) (Eicher 2002, 38). In fact, Chile's textbook case of extension privatization has shown that after twenty-four years of experimenting with privatizing the delivery of extension, the extension system was still dependent on the annual political decision to allocate public resources to pay for 85 to 90 percent of the US$22 million annual cost of extension (Berdegue and Marchant 2002, 26). Moreover, the World Bank's recent Workshop on Extension reviewed thirty-four country studies of extension reform and concluded, "the public sector must continue to be a major player, both in funding and coordinating operations" (World Bank 2003).

❼ *Incentives for Knowledge Workers.* The monetary and non-monetary gap between public and NGO extension is large and smoldering. Since front-line extension workers are paid relatively low salaries (US$100 per month for certificate to US$200 per month for diploma holders), DNER should request donors to finance the construction of several hundred houses and provide motorcycles[10] to interested extensionists on long-term purchase contracts similar to those developed by CLUSA (1999).

❽ *Extension Partnerships.* Extension partnerships are currently under-developed at the national and provincial levels. The challenge for DNER is to build horizontal and working partnerships with the IIAM and with the zonal research centers. In order to promote extension and research synergies, we recommend changing the proposed Provincial Extension Management Committee (DNER 2002a) to the Provincial Extension and Research Management Committee in order to increase the connectivity between extension and research.[11]

❾ *Market Information and Marketing.* The ninth challenge is the need for DNER to develop stronger links with organizations generating market information such as SIMA, the policy analysis team in the Ministry of Agriculture, the FAO, IFPRI, and others working on value-added commodities (Kherallah et al. 2002). Competitiveness in global markets is a critical challenge to agricultural research and extension services because African agricultural exports have declined dramatically from 8.6 percent of world agricultural exports in 1961 to 3.0 percent in 1996 (Binswanger and Lutz 2001). The challenge is for extension, research, and market information specialists to ferret out new regional and global markets and help the family sector generate new income streams from the sale of value-added commodities such as sesame, paprika, and fruits and vegetables in national, regional, and global markets (Benfica et al. 2002). DNER should review the research that the Ministry of Agriculture has underway on agribusiness and market development and join forces with DAP, SIMA,[12] and CLUSA on future studies (Ruotsi 2003).

⑩ *Impact Studies.* The tenth challenge is the need for DNER to work closely with the new Socio-Economic Research unit in IIAM and the Policy Analysis Department to design studies of the economics of alternative extension models, technology assessment, and diffusion. A high-priority study is measuring the impact and economics of new extension models such as the Farmers Field Schools (FFS) model, which has achieved mixed success in Asia. [13] One of the questions to address is: Why has the cost of FFS programs being implemented by Word Vision International in Mozambique been higher than those in Asia? (Danida 2002a). Another issue is measuring whether FFS training results in increasing the knowledge of farmers about farming practices and whether farmers are using this knowledge to increase farm productivity.[14]

DNER should encourage the new socio-economic research unit in IAAM to carry out impact studies of selected food crops (e.g. cassava and quality protein maize), new cash crops for export, as well as fish culture, livestock, and irrigation. The results of these impact studies will inform the Ministry of Agriculture, the Ministry of Finance, members of Parliament and donors of the cost, benefits, and impact of public investments in extension and research.

## NOTES

1. Mozambique's first Extension Master Plan contended, "Over the long-term . . . the amount of government resources allocated to extension and the number of publicly financed extension workers will decrease as the private sector and civil society develop. . . ." (DNER 1997, 33).

2. In early 2005, DNER had 770 extension workers and managers, NGOs had 840, and private farms employed 228 for a total of 1,838 extension workers in Mozambique.

3. Appendix 1 indicates the low educational level of public extension workers by province.

4. Brazil—the world's new breadbasket—has some important lessons for Mozambique. Back in the 1960s, Brazil made a high-level political decision to build a strong agricultural science base and some new agricultural universities. After four decades of sustained institution building, Brazil is now an agricultural superpower and 40 percent of its exports in 2004 were agricultural products. Brazil is now the world's leading exporter of beef, chickens, and orange juice.

5. An NGO representative in Maputo speculated that the public extension workers were probably receiving per diem for their day-to-day work in their villages and that these per diem payments would substantially narrow the financial gap between public and NGO extension workers. But front-line extension workers do not receive per diem for their day-to-day work in the villages (Eicher 2002).

6. A supervisory mission to Gaza province discovered that twenty motorcycles that had been given to DNER agents were in need of repair in the Manjacaze district (DNER 2002).

7. See Rusike et al. (2004) per a discussion of the results of four years of research on the implementation of the FFS model in Zimbabwe.

8. Critical issues in developing a professional extension service include expanding opportunities for training, and making housing and motorcycles available to front-line extension workers.

9. Table 3 and appendix 2 can be of great help in this exercise.

10. The housing and motorcycle issues are included in the second Extension Master Plan for 2005–9 (DNER 2004).

11. This type of joint research/extension committee should not be established at the district level. For example, it would be impossible for Mozambique's sole maize breeder to meet with extension workers in one-third or one-half of the sixty-six districts where DNER was functioning in 2004.

12. See Mabota et al. (2003).

13. At the farm level in Asia, the FFS program teaches farmers how to manage their rice plots as ecosystems, carefully maintaining the balance between pests and their natural predators and reverting to pesticides only when the pests are getting out of hand (Roling and Pretty 1997). For a critical review of the FFS extension programs in the Philippines and Indonesia, see Quizon et al. (2001); Rola et al. (2002); and Feder et al. (2004).

14. A recent study of the impact of farmer field-school training on knowledge and productivity among farmers in Peru concluded that the average knowledge of farmers about

technical issues increased in the short run, but the authors had no direct observations to measure the impact of increased knowledge on farm productivity (Gotland et al. 2004).

# CHAPTER 8

# Summary and Conclusions

gricultural extension is now in disarray throughout Africa after a period of rapid expansion and high expectations from the sixties to the early nineties. The number of extension workers in Africa increased from 21,000 in 1959 to 57,000 in 1980 (Judd, Boyce, and Evenson 1986). Likewise, the World Bank provided US$3 billion in direct support of agricultural extension in developing countries since 1981 (World Bank 2004). However, Swanson (2004) reports that with a few exceptions, donor support for extension had dried up by the mid nineties.

Why has donor support to agricultural extension declined in Africa? There are three basic reasons. First, many of the extension models imported from other continents have not been productive and financially sustainable under African conditions. Second, most academic and donor experts in extension have underestimated the time and continuity of national and donor funding that it takes to build productive and financially sustainable national agricultural extension systems in Africa. Third, history has shown that in many countries extension workers lack access to a steady flow of new agricultural technology that can raise smallholder crop yields and farm profitability on a recurring basis.

Africa's experience over the past four decades has shown that an army of agricultural extension workers and NGOs have been unable by themselves to transform African agriculture and deliver Green Revolutions to African farmers. Agricultural research is the driving force for generating new technology for extension workers who have a strategic role to play in speeding up the adoption of new technology as well as providing information on health, marketing and nutrition to village people. Because of complementary between research and extension, extension strategies and priorities should be developed in close cooperation with agricultural research organizations. But, it is also important for both research and extension in Mozambique to be closely interlinked with faculties of agriculture because the faculties are needed to replenish the stock of human capital in research and extension organizations over time. To summarize, these examples illustrate the need for managers and scientists in research, extension, and agricultural higher education to communicate and cooperate even if the are administratively responsible to different ministries.

Getting the family sector (small-scale farms) moving is the acid test for the political, scientific and private sector leadership of Mozambique. Since Mozambique is an agrarian-dominated country, there is a need for the government to take the lead in crafting and building a system of agricultural development institutions to help the family sector increase agricultural productivity, and meet family and national food security needs. But to achieve these goals, political leadership is needed to ensure that Mozambican and donor funds are wisely invested in the three core agricultural institutions—agricultural research, extension and faculties of agriculture—for the long pull, i.e. the coming twenty to twenty-five years. Africa's development experience since independence painfully reminds us that there are no quick fixes in building the institutional foundation for a modern agriculture. The challenge ahead for Mozambique is learning how to pragmatically craft a system of institutions, public and private, that will help put more money into the pockets of smallholders and improve family and national food security.

This study has focused on building a national agricultural extension system for the "particular case" of Mozambique. Although Mozambique became independent in 1975, it did not set up a national public extension system until 1987. We have analyzed the evolution of agricultural extension in Mozambique from 1987 until the completion of the first Extension Master Plan in 2004. This study also examines the changing roles of the three main providers of extension in Mozambique: public, NGO and private—during three phases of extension development from 1987 to 2004. We contend that the challenge ahead for MADER and the donor community is to slowly upgrade the size and quality of the public extension system (DNER) because it is the cornerstone of Mozambique's pluralistic extension system and it is the logical institution to replace international NGOs when, foreign aid, the main current source of funding for international NGOs, is phased out.

This study has analyzed the evolution of agricultural extension in Mozambique from 1987 to 2004. The study starts with the premise that the role and sequencing of extension in Africa should be conceptualized as part of an interactive agricultural knowledge triangle, which is composed of research, extension, and agricultural higher education. Because of Africa's seven different colonial histories, it follows that crafting national extension systems should draw on past experience, pilot studies, learning by doing and emerging opportunities at home and in global markets.

But there are no blueprints for strengthening extension systems in Africa. Rather, the development of an efficient and financially sustainable agricultural extension system for Mozambique requires pilot studies, experimentation with institutional innovations and learning from the experience of other countries such as Uganda (Nahdy, Byekwaso, and Nielson 2002). Mozambique has made a wise decision to support a pragmatic approach to outsourcing extension by carrying out pilot studies of outsourcing in two districts. The DNER and EU outsourcing experiments now underway will help Mozambique learn from its own experience whether to continue outsourcing or phase it out.

We have observed that donor agencies and international organizations have a tendency to recommend and finance general policy and institutional prescriptions for all of Africa such as structural adjustment programs, the U.S. land-grant university model and the T&V and the Farmer Field Schools extension models. But Africa is a large and complex continent of fifty-four nations at variable stages of institutional development. Several examples illustrate the failure of general institutional and policy prescriptions for all of Africa. The T&V extension model was implemented in several dozen countries in Africa and subsequently rejected because it cost 25 to 40 percent higher than the models it replaced and it was found to be financially unsustainable. Likewise structural adjustment programs have not achieved their expected rates of economic growth. Finally the U.S. land-grant type of university has floundered in Africa.

This study argues that policy makers and donors should discontinue the promotion of general prescriptions of downsizing, outsourcing and privatizing extension and instead focus on the particular case of a country such as Mozambique. The challenge then is to craft models of agricultural extension for Mozambique through a pragmatic process of learning by doing and learning from the African and global experience. Mozambique represents a particular case in institution building because its public extension service (DNER) is only seventeen years old and it is a relatively lean organization of 770 public extension workers and managers working in 66 of the 128 districts in the country. NGOs (local and international) employed 840 extensionists and private (large-scale) farms collectively employed 228 extension workers for a grand total of 1,838 in extensionists in early 2005. However, the challenges facing public extension in Mozambique are awesome. For example, the incentive structure of front line public extension workers is unacceptably low, the job insecurity of extensionists on temporary contracts is debilitating and the quality of Mozambique's human capital in agricultural research and extension is inadequate for a country of 19 million people and a large but untapped agricultural potential.

One of the important findings of this study is that false assumptions have kept public agricultural extension in Mozambique "on hold" over the past five years. For example, the first Extension Master Plan (DNER 1997) recommended that the size of DNER be capped at 800 extension workers. Why has public extension been kept on hold during the 1999–2004 period? We think it is partially because Mozambique has uncritically followed the general prescription of many donors to "free agriculture from the state," outsource extension to the private sector and assume that poor farmers can buy their way out of poverty by paying for the services of private extension agents and thereby reduce the size of the public extension service and public funding of extension. The first Extension Master Plan covering 1999 to 2004 adhered to this line of thinking and assumed that, over time, the private sector would replace public extensionists and cost sharing would reduce total government expenditure on extension.

Mozambique has much to learn from Brazil's experience in building a system of articulated and interconnected agricultural institutions that make up the agricultural knowledge triangle. Some 40 years ago Brazil took a high level political decision to build a strong human capital base and a globally competitive agricultural science base (Macedo et al. 2003). Brazil mobilized high-level political support to increase its public investments in both agricultural research and extension. The government wisely viewed researchers and extension workers as valuable knowledge workers who could draw on their "global human capital chains" to exchange ideas and generate public goods (new technology and knowledge) that were made available free of charge to Brazilian farmers. To summarize, Brazil is now an agricultural superpower because it took a political decision some forty years ago to build a strong national agricultural science base and an efficient technology delivery system in an accretionary (step-by-step) manner over a period of four decades.

Without question, DNER should hire a few Subject Matter Specialists (SMSs) in marketing to help Mozambican farmers generate new income streams (e.g., paprika, pigeon peas, tobacco) in a globally competitive agricultural economy. But SMSs in agricultural marketing must be well rewarded (in monetary and non- monetary terms) because there is a global market for these "knowledge workers" and they can move from country to country and continent to continent. Kenya found this out when Viet Nam hired its star coffee breeder and drew on his decades of experience to help jump-start Viet Nam's coffee production and exports. Increased investment in coffee breeding and a number of policy and marketing reforms elevated Viet Nam from the 42nd largest coffee exporter in the world in 1994 to the lofty position as the second largest coffee exporter (after Brazil) in 2004.

This study argues that increased local and donor support is needed for both public research and extension because agricultural extension workers and NGOs by themselves cannot generate Green Revolutions in Africa. Investment in agricultural research has a critical role to play in generating Green Revolutions. The new Socio-Economic Research Unit that has been proposed for IIAM (the national agricultural research organization) will be staffed with a small number of socio-economists and extension researchers. This research and extension partnership will help improve the connectivity between research and extension by carrying out urgently- needed impact studies to guide agricultural research priorities, technology development and diffusion.

To be sure, the current donor preoccupation with extension decentralization, participation, outsourcing and cost sharing is both appealing and seductive. However, both public and private investments are needed to achieve these multiple goals of decentralization, participation and giving voice to farmers and rural communities which will help speed up accountability and performance from local extension agents. These demand pressures are critical in serving as performance checks on extension managers and field staff. The mix of public and private investments in extension will vary over time. However, even if local NGOs and private consulting firms would expand their capacity to offer extension services to farmers, the public treasury will likely have to pay a large share of the extension bill for decades to come in a poor country such as Mozambique. It is important to note that the World Bank's new rural development strategy reports that, "Extension services will have to be publicly financed in the poorest countries" (World Bank 2003b, 47).

To summarize, the challenge for Mozambique over the next ten to fifteen years is to focus and concentrate on strengthening and gradually expanding the size and improving the quality, accountability and relevance of DNER (public extension) which is the cornerstone of Mozambique's pluralistic extension system (Rivera and Alex 2004). NGOs and large-scale private farms can supplement but not replace the necessary role of public extension at this early stage of Mozambique's institutional development.

We have identified three system-wide problems and ten challenges facing the Ministry of Agriculture and Rural Development and DNER. Without question, these are going to be difficult challenges to resolve. Some hard choices and changes must be made at the bottom and at the top of the extension system. At the top of the system, the role of the managers of the central office of DNER should be shifted from managing the implementation of the national public extension system to providing the vision and strategic thinking on building the human capital base for an effective national extension system, setting quality standards, making the case to expand extension in high potential areas, improving the coordination of public, private and NGO extension, and developing horizontal partnerships with marketing specialists, universities and the private sector and carrying out M&E for the national system. At the bottom, the challenge is to continue to push extension implementation decisions down to districts in order to give farmers a voice and help them generate farmer-led demand pressure on the extension and research priority settings.

To summarize, the 3.3 million small-scale farms in Mozambique will have a hard time "buying their way out of poverty" by paying for extension services. Public investments in agricultural research, extension, and faculties and schools of agriculture are needed to produce public goods (information, knowledge and technology) for distribution to all people, with special emphasis on small-scale farmers. The bottom line is the need for Mozambicans to develop a national extension system that meets the needs of the "particular case of Mozambique."

# Number of Public Extension Personnel by Province, Educational Level, and Employment Status: 2004

| PROVINCE | EDUCATION LEVEL | EXISTING MANPOWER | | | | | | | | |
| | | BY EMPLOYMENT STATUS AND SEX | | | | | | TOTAL BY SEX | | TOTAL EXISTING MANPOWER |
| | | CONTRACT | | | CIVIL SERVANT | | | | | |
| | | MALE | FEMALE | SUBTOTAL | MALE | FEMALE | SUBTOTAL | MALE | FEMALE | |
| MAPUTO | First degree and above | 1 | | 1 | | 1 | 1 | 1 | 1 | 2 |
| | Diploma | 27 | 6 | 33 | 6 | 4 | 10 | 33 | 10 | 43 |
| | Certificate | 0 | 0 | 0 | 7 | | 7 | 7 | 0 | 7 |
| | Below certificate | 0 | 0 | 0 | 0 | 0 | 0 | 0 | 0 | 0 |
| | TOTAL | 28 | 6 | 34 | 13 | 5 | 18 | 41 | 11 | 52 |
| GAZA | First degree and above | | | | 2 | | 2 | 2 | 0 | 2 |
| | Diploma | 10 | 33 | 43 | | | 28 | 61 | 10 | 71 |
| | Certificate | | | | | | | 0 | 0 | 0 |
| | Below certificate | | | | | | | 0 | 0 | 0 |
| | TOTAL | 10 | 33 | 43 | 2 | 0 | 30 | 63 | 10 | 73 |
| INHAMBANE | First degree and above | 0 | 0 | 0 | 0 | 0 | 0 | 0 | 0 | 0 |
| | Diploma | 45 | 3 | 48 | 3 | 1 | 4 | 48 | 4 | 52 |
| | Certificate | 0 | 0 | 0 | 2 | 0 | 2 | 2 | 0 | 2 |
| | Below certificate | 0 | 0 | 0 | 0 | 0 | 0 | 0 | 0 | 0 |
| | TOTAL | 45 | 3 | 48 | 5 | 1 | 6 | 50 | 4 | 54 |
| SOFALA | First degree and above | 6 | 1 | 7 | 1 | 0 | 1 | 7 | 1 | 8 |
| | Diploma | 43 | 1 | 44 | 7 | 0 | 7 | 50 | 1 | 51 |
| | Certificate | 0 | 0 | 0 | 19 | 2 | 21 | 19 | 2 | 21 |
| | Below certificate | 0 | 0 | 0 | 6 | 0 | 6 | 6 | 0 | 6 |
| | TOTAL | 49 | 2 | 51 | 33 | 2 | 35 | 82 | 4 | 86 |

| PROVINCE | EDUCATION LEVEL | EXISTING MANPOWER | | | | | | TOTAL BY SEX | | TOTAL |
| | | BY EMPLOYMENT STATUS AND SEX | | | | | | | | EXISTING |
| | | CONTRACT | | | CIVIL SERVANT | | | | | MANPOWER |
| | | MALE | FEMALE | SUBTOTAL | MALE | FEMALE | SUBTOTAL | MALE | FEMALE | |
|---|---|---|---|---|---|---|---|---|---|---|
| MANICA | First degree and above | 1 | 1 | 2 | 1 | | 1 | 2 | 1 | 3 |
| | Diploma | 36 | 2 | 38 | 4 | 1 | 5 | 40 | 3 | 43 |
| | Certificate | 14 | 1 | 15 | | | | 14 | 1 | 15 |
| | Below certificate | 1 | 0 | 1 | | | | 1 | 0 | 1 |
| | TOTAL | 52 | 4 | 56 | 5 | 1 | 6 | 57 | 5 | 62 |
| TETE | First degree and above | 2 | 0 | 2 | 0 | 0 | 0 | 2 | 0 | 2 |
| | Diploma | 25 | 0 | 25 | 2 | 0 | 2 | 27 | 0 | 27 |
| | Certificate | 0 | 0 | 0 | 13 | 6 | 19 | 13 | 6 | 19 |
| | Below certificate | 0 | 0 | 0 | 8 | 0 | 8 | 8 | 0 | 8 |
| | TOTAL | 27 | 0 | 27 | 23 | 6 | 29 | 50 | 6 | 56 |
| ZAMBEZIA | First degree and above | 2 | 0 | 2 | 0 | 0 | 0 | 2 | 0 | 2 |
| | Diploma | 36 | 7 | 43 | 0 | 0 | 0 | 36 | 7 | 43 |
| | Certificate | 8 | 2 | 10 | 0 | 0 | 0 | 8 | 2 | 10 |
| | Below certificate | 0 | 0 | 0 | 0 | 0 | 0 | 0 | 0 | 0 |
| | TOTAL | 46 | 9 | 55 | 0 | 0 | 0 | 46 | 9 | 55 |
| NAMPULA | First degree and above | 3 | | 3 | 1 | | 1 | 4 | 0 | 4 |
| | Diploma | 33 | 1 | 34 | 1 | | 1 | 34 | 1 | 35 |
| | Certificate | 72 | 3 | 75 | | | | 72 | 3 | 75 |
| | Below certificate | 6 | | 6 | 1 | | 1 | 7 | 0 | 7 |
| | TOTAL | 114 | 4 | 118 | 3 | 0 | 3 | 117 | 4 | 121 |
| C. DELGADO | First degree and above | 1 | | 1 | | | | 1 | 0 | 1 |
| | Diploma | 30 | | 30 | | | | 30 | 0 | 30 |
| | Certificate | 58 | 2 | 60 | | | | 58 | 2 | 60 |
| | Below certificate | | | | | | | 0 | 0 | 0 |
| | TOTAL | 89 | 2 | 91 | | | | 89 | 2 | 91 |
| NIASSA | First degree and above | 4 | 0 | 4 | 0 | 0 | 0 | 4 | 0 | 4 |
| | Diploma | 16 | 2 | 18 | 3 | 0 | 3 | 19 | 2 | 21 |
| | Certificate | 2 | 0 | 2 | 15 | 0 | 15 | 17 | 0 | 17 |
| | Below certificate | 0 | 0 | 0 | 16 | 0 | 16 | 16 | 0 | 16 |
| | TOTAL | 22 | 2 | 24 | 34 | 0 | 34 | 56 | 2 | 58 |
| TOTAL | First degree and above | 20 | 2 | 22 | 5 | 1 | 6 | 25 | 3 | 28 |
| | Diploma | 301 | 55 | 356 | 26 | 6 | 60 | 378 | 38 | 416 |
| | Certificate | 154 | 8 | 162 | 56 | 8 | 64 | 210 | 16 | 226 |
| | Below certificate | 7 | 0 | 7 | 31 | 0 | 31 | 38 | 0 | 38 |
| | TOTAL | 482 | 65 | 547 | 118 | 15 | 161 | 651 | 57 | 708 |

Source: DNER 2004

# Extension Coverage by National and International NGOs and Private Firms by Province: 2004

| NGO | | AREA OF OPERATION | | PERSONNEL | |
|---|---|---|---|---|---|
| | | PROVINCE | DISTRICT | TOTAL | EXTENSIONISTS |
| NATIONAL NGO | | | | | |
| 1 | ACRIDEC | Gaza | | 1 | 0 |
| 2 | ADAP/SF | Nampula | Nampula e Mecuburi | 7 | 5 |
| 3 | ADCR | Gaza | Chigubo | 5 | 2 |
| 4 | ADEL | Sofala | Nhamatanda e Caia | 4 | 0 |
| 5 | AJDR | Nampula | Nampula/Rapale, Mecuburi e Murrupula | 4 | 2 |
| 6 | APDICOMA | Maputo | Manhiça | 24 | 16 |
| 7 | Associação Progresso | Niassa | Lago, Lichinga, Muembe e Sanga | | |
| 8 | ATAP | Maputo | Boane, Manhiça, Magude | | |
| 9 | Caritas de Moçambique | Gaza | Chicualacuala, Chigubo, Chokwe, Guijá, Mabalane, Massangena e Massingir | 8 | 3 |
| | CARITAS DIOCESANA | Inahambane | Zavala, Panda, Inharrime, Morrumbene, Vilanculo, Inhassoro e Cidade I´bane | 9 | 8 |
| | Caritas Diocesanas | Zambezia | Mopeia | | |
| | Caritas Messicas | Manica | Manica | 10 | 6 |
| 10 | Casa do Gaiato | Maputo | Boane, Namaacha | 3 | 0 |
| 11 | CCM | Zambezia | Gurue, Namarro, Milange, Mopeia e Nicoadala | 30 | 20 |

| NGO | | AREA OF OPERATION | | PERSONNEL | |
|---|---|---|---|---|---|
| | | PROVINCE | DISTRICT | TOTAL | EXTENSIONISTS |
| | CCM (Gurue) | Zambezia | Gurue | 7 | 6 |
| 12 | COBAREMA | Tete | Tsangano, Changara e Tete-cidade | 36 | 5 |
| 13 | Estamos | Niassa | Mandimba | 7 | 4 |
| 14 | FDC | Gaza | Bilene e Chokwe | 8 | 7 |
| 15 | Fórum Terra | Nampula | Muecate, Mecuburi, Erati, Mogovolas, Murrupula | | |
| 16 | KEAGOZA SIMUKAI | Manica | Manica | 13 | 4 |
| 17 | Kulima | Zambezia | Gile, Inhassunge e Chinde | 12 | 10 |
| | KULIMA | Nampula | Memba, Erati e Nacala Velha | 17 | 12 |
| | KULIMA Kulukulu | Maputo | Marracuene, Moamba | 27 | 24 |
| | KULIMA/AAA | Inahambane | Vilanculo, Mabote | 7 | 0 |
| 18 | Kutsemba | Maputo | Matutuine | 6 | 3 |
| 19 | MAHLAHLE | Inahambane | Massinga, Zavala e I'bane | 5 | 2 |
| 20 | Movimundo | Niassa | Mandimba | 13 | 7 |
| 21 | Olipa – ODES | Nampula | Nampula/Rapale, Murrupula, Mecuburi, Ribaue, Lalaua e Malema | | |
| 22 | ORAM | Gaza | Boane, Manhiça, Matutuine | | |
| | ORAM | Gaza | Chokwé, Guijá, Bilene, Chibuto, Manjacaze, Massingir, Xai-Xai | 16 | 8 |
| | ORAM | Nampula | Angoche, Moma, Monapo, Nacala Velha, Erati, Mecuburi, Meconta, Malema, Murrupula, Ribaue, Mogovolas, Mongicual, Memba e Nacaroa | 44 | 10 |
| 23 | PRODER | Sofala | Gorongosa, Cheringoma, Maringue, Muanza, Caia e Chemba | | |
| 24 | Qualicajú | Nampula | Nampula, Rapale, Mossuril e Mogicual | 40 | 0 |
| 25 | Quinta Mecuasse | Nampula | Ribaue e Malema | | |
| 26 | Reconstruindo Esperança | Maputo | Manhiça | | |
| 27 | Red Cross of Mazambique | Tete | Changare e Chiuta | 2 | 0 |
| 28 | UCA | Niassa | Lichinga e Sanga | | |
| 29 | UCAMA | Manica | Sussundenga, Manica, Gondola, Chimoio/Cidade, Mossurize e Barué | 17 | 17 |
| 30 | UCASN | Niassa | Cuamba, Mandimba, Macanhelas e Metarica | 29 | 19 |
| 31 | UMOKAZI | C. Delgado | Mecufi, Metuge, Nangade, Macomia, Moeda, Chiúre e Quissanga | 49 | 34 |
| 32 | Vukoxa | Gaza | Chokwe | 78 | 5 |
| 33 | AMODESE | Maputo | Manhiça | | |
| 34 | AMREF | Maputo | Manhiça | | |

| NGO | AREA OF OPERATION | | PERSONNEL | |
|---|---|---|---|---|
| | PROVINCE | DISTRICT | TOTAL | EXTENSIONISTS |
| 35 AMRU | Maputo | Magude | | |
| 36 CREDEC | Maputo | Boane | | |
| 37 Hiphuneni | Maputo | Boane | | |
| 38 INTERMOL | Maputo | Matutuíne | | |
| 39 UNGC | Maputo | Moamba | | |

**INTERNATIONAL NGO**

| | NGO | PROVINCE | DISTRICT | TOTAL | EXTENSIONISTS |
|---|---|---|---|---|---|
| 1 | World Relief | Gaza | Chokwe, Guijá, Mabalane, Massingir e Xai-Xai | 6 | |
| 2 | ACDI/VOCA | Manica | Sussundenga, Gondola, Manica e Chimoio | 20 | 16 |
| 3 | ACORD | Niassa | LAGO e Sanga | | |
| 4 | Action aid | Maputo | Manhiça, Marracuene | | |
| 5 | ADRA | Gaza | Chibuto e Manjacaze | 15 | 9 |
| | ADRA | Inahambane | Homoine, Jangamo, Inharrime e Zavala | 33 | 20 |
| | ADRA | Zambezia | Mocuba, Ile e Maganja da Costa | 22 | 19 |
| 6 | AFRICARE | Manica | Gondola, Sussundenga, manica e Barue | 11 | 9 |
| 7 | AFSC | Manica | Manica | | |
| 8 | Aga Khan Foundation | C. Delgado | Quissanga, Ibo, Meluco, Macomia e Pemba Metuge | 11 | 8 |
| 9 | Ajuda Popular da Noroega | Tete | Marávia e Chifunde | | |
| 10 | CARE | Nampula | Murrupula | 8 | 6 |
| 11 | CARE internacional | Inahambane | Vilanculo, Inhassoro, Mabote e Govuro | 28 | 19 |
| 12 | CARE Internacional (VIDA I) | Nampula | Malema, Ribaué, Lalaua | 15 | 12 |
| | CARE Internacional (VIDA II) | Nampula | Angoche, Moma, Mogovolas, Nampula, Meconta, Muecate, Monapo, Nacaroa, Erati | 120 | 54 |
| 13 | CLUSA | Niassa | Cuamba, Maúa e Marrupa | | |
| 14 | Concern Universal | Niassa | Lichinga, Cuamba, Sanga, Muembe, Nipepe, Majune e Lago | | |
| 15 | FOS Chitima | Tete | Cahora-Bassa(Chitima) | 6 | 4 |
| 16 | HEIFER MOZAMBIQUE (H.P.I) | Zambezia | Mopeia, Morrumbala, Nicoadala, Maganja da Costa, Mocuba, Ile, Molocue e Lugela | 9 | 6 |
| 17 | Helvetas | Maputo | Boane, Matutuine, Magude, Moamba | 4 | 3 |
| | Helvetas | C. Delgado | Chiúre, Ancuambe, Namuno e Balama | 11 | 9 |
| 18 | Hope for Africa Missons | Gaza | Chokwe | 3 | 2 |
| 19 | IUCN | Maputo | Matutuine | | |
| 20 | Lutheran World Federation | Sofala | Chibabava e Buzi | 22 | 0 |
| | Lutheran World Federation | Tete | | | |

| NGO | | AREA OF OPERATION | | PERSONNEL | |
|---|---|---|---|---|---|
| | | PROVINCE | DISTRICT | TOTAL | EXTENSIONISTS |
| 21 | OIKOS | Maputo | Magude | | |
| | OIKOS | Gaza | Bilene | 6 | 5 |
| | OIKOS | Niassa | Lichinga e Mandimba | 12 | 4 |
| 22 | OXFAM GB | Niassa | Maua, Metarica, Cuamba, Macanhelas, Mandimba | 18 | 10 |
| 23 | Programa MAMM/UDC | Nampula | Moma, Angoche, Mongicual e Mogovolas | 13 | 9 |
| 24 | Save the Children | Gaza | Bilene, Chibuto, Manjacaze e Xai-Xai | 4 | 3 |
| 25 | Vetaid | Gaza | Chicualacuala, Chigubo, Mabalane e Massangena | 22 | 15 |
| 26 | World Relief-Sempre verde | Niassa | Cuamba, Mecanhelas, Metarica, Maúa, Nipepe, Marrupa, Lichinga, Sanga, Ngaúma, Muembé, Majune, Lagos e Mandimba | 56 | 46 |
| 27 | World Vision | Gaza | Manjacaze | 5 | 3 |
| | World Vision | Tete | Cahora-Bassa(Chitima) | 10 | 9 |
| | World Vision | Zambezia | Inhassunge, Nicoadala, Namacura, Mopeia, Morrumbala, Lugela, Namarroi, Gurue, Alto Molocué e Gilé | 133 | 106 |
| | World Vision | Nampula | Mossuril, Ilha de Moçambique e Mongicuala | 23 | 19 |
| 28 | FHI | Sofala | | NA | 51 |
| 29 | CARITAS | Sofala | | NA | 12 |
| 30 | PROMEC | Sofala | | NA | 3 |

PARTNERSHIP

| 31 | KULIMA/Visao Mundial | Inahambane | Zavala e Inharrime | 8 | 4 |
|---|---|---|---|---|---|
| 32 | KULIMA/VETAID | Inahambane | Zavala, Jangamo e Inharrime | 5 | |

PRIVATE FIRMS

| 1 | Mozambique Leaf Tobacco | Tete | Angónia, Tsangano, Marávia, Macanga, Moatize, Chiúta e Zumbo | 80 | 80 |
|---|---|---|---|---|---|
| 2 | Diamond (Tabaco de Tete) | Tete | Chifunde, Cahora-Bassa e Changara | 7 | 7 |
| 3 | Dunavant Moç, Lda | Tete | Moatize, Marávia, Chifunde, Zumbo, Macanga e Chiúta | | |
| 4 | Tabaco de Tete | Tete | Chinde,Cahora-Bassa e Changara | 85 | 85 |
| 5 | Agema | Zambezia | Nicoadala | 10 | 8 |
| 6 | Tabacos de Moçambique Ltd. | Niassa | Mandimba, Memba, Mecanhelas, Maúa, Metarica, Marrupa | 68 | 28 |
| 7 | Mecotex, Ida | Zambezia | Mocuba, Maganja da Costa, Lugela e Ile | 9 | 8 |
| 8 | PLEXUS | C. Delgado | Ancuabe, Montepuez, Namuno, Balama, Meluco, Quissanga, Macomia, Mueda, Muidumbe e Nangabe | 107 | 12 |

# References

Abrahamsson, Hans, and Anders Nilsson 1994. *Moçambique em transição: Um estudo da história de desenvolvimento durante o período 1974–1992.* Padrigu. CEEI-ISRI (Segunda edição). Goteborg. Suécia.

Alex, Gary, Willem Zijp, Derek Byerlee, and others. 2002. *Rural extension and advisory services: New directions.* Rural Development Strategy Background Paper No. 9. Washington D.C.: World Bank.

Anderson, Jock R., and Gershon Feder. 2004. Agricultural extension: Good intentions and hard realities. *The World Bank Research Observer* 19(1): 41–60.

Bagchee, Arun. 1994. *Agricultural extension in Africa.* Washington D.C.: World Bank.

Beintema, Nienke, A.F.D. Auila, and P.G. Pardey. 2001. *Agricultural R and D in Brazil: Policy, investments and institutional profile,* June. Washington. D.C.: IFPRI.

Beintema, Nienke, E. Modiakgotla, and L. Mazhani. 2004. *Botswana. Asti country brief,* No. 19. Washington D.C.: IFPRI and DAR.

Benfica, Rui. M.S., David Tschirley, and Liria Sambo. 2002. Agro-industry and smallholder agriculture: Institutional arrangements and rural poverty reduction in Mozambique. In *Flash*, No 33E, 10 November. Maputo: Ministry of Agriculture and Rural Development.

Benor, Daniel, and J. Harrison. 1977. *Agricultural extension: The training and visit system.* Washington D.C.: World Bank.

Berdegue, Julio A., and Cristian Marchant. 2002. Chile: The evolution of the agricultural advisory service for small farmers: 1978–2000. In *Contracting for agricultural extension: International case studies and emerging practices*, edited by W.M. Rivera and W. Zijp, 21–27. New York: CABI Publishing.

Berdegue, Julio, Thomas Reardon, and German Escobar. 2002. The increasing importance of nonagricultural rural employment and income." In *Development of rural economies in Latin America and the Caribbean*, edited by Ruben G. Echeverria, 159–86. Washington, D.C..: Inter-American Development Bank.

Bias, Calisto, and Cynthia Donovan. 2003. Gaps and opportunities for agricultural sector development in Mozambique. Research Report No. 54E, April. Maputo: MADER/DE Research Paper Series.

BIFAD. 2003. Renewing USAID investment in global long-term training and capacity building in agriculture and rural development. Washington, D.C.: Board for International Food and Agricultural Development.

Binswanger, Hans, and Ernst Lutz. 2001. Agricultural trade barriers, trade negotiations and the interests of developing counties. In *Tomorrow's agriculture: Incentives, institutions, infrastructure and innovations*, Proceedings of The Twenty-Fourth International Conference of Agricultural Economists, Berlin, 13–18 August 2000, edited by G.H. Peters and Prabhu Pingali. Burlington, Vt.: Ashgate.

Boletim da República. 1987. Publicação oficial da república popular de Moçambique. I SÉRIE–Número 2. Diploma Ministerial n. 41/87.Maputo. 1987/83/25

Bonnen, J.T. 1998. Agricultural development: Transforming human capital, technology and institutions. In *International Agricultural Development*, 3d ed., edited by C.K. Eicher and J.M. Staatz, 271–86. Baltimore: Johns Hopkins University Press.

Boughton, Duncan et al. 2002. Cotton sector policies and performance in sub-Saharan Africa: Lessons behind the numbers in Mozambique and Zambia. *Flash*, No. 34E, 10 December. Directorate of Economics. Maputo: MADER.

Byerlee, Derek, and Edith Hesse Polanco. 1986. Farmers' stepwise adoption of technological packages: Evidence from the Mexican Altiplano. *Americal Journal of Agricultural Economics* 68(1): 519–27.

Byerlee, Derek, and Ken Fischer. 2002. Accessing modern science: Policy and institutional options for agricultural biotechnology in developing countries. *World Development* 30(6): 931–48.

Campbell, Dustan A., and St. Clair Barker. 1997. Selecting appropriate content and methods in programme delivery. In *Improving Agricultural Extension. A Reference Manual*, edited by Burton E. Swanson, Robert P. Bentz, and Andrew J. Sofranko. Rome: FAO.

Carr, Marilyn ed. 1991. *Women and food security. The experience of SADC countries.* London: Intermediate Technology Publications.

CLUSA. 1999. Contrato de compra de uma motorizada. 11 June. CLUSA: Nampula.

———. 2001. Mozambique: Rural group enterprise development program. Work Plan. November 2001–October 2002, Nampula: Cooperative League of the USA.

Coulter, Jonathan, Tiago Wandschneider, and Fernando Carvalheira. 2004. Study on contract farming and supply chain financing in Mozambique. Draft. August. London: Natural Resources Institute.

Crowder, L. Van, and Jon Anderson. 2001. Contracting for extension services: contrasting approaches from Mozambique. In *Agricultural extension systems: An international perspective*, edited by Frank L. Brewer, 112–24. North Chelmsford, Mass.: Erudition Books.

Crowder, L. Van, and Jon Anderson. 2002. Uganda: Private sector secondment of government extension agents. In *Contracting for agricultural extension. International case studies and emerging practices*, edited by William M. Rivera and Willem Zijp, 155–62. New York: CABI Publishing.

DANIDA. 2002. Review of Danida-supported extension and research activities within the agricultural sector programme support (ASPS): Mozambique. June. Copenhagen, Denmark: DANIDA.

———. 2002a. Promotion, development and implementation of the IPM approach within the agricultural sector in Mozambique. Technical Backstopping Mission. June. Copenhagen, Denmark: DANIDA.

———. 2002b. Evaluation: The agricultural development project in Tete, Mozambique: An impact study. September. Copenhagen, Denmark: DANIDA.

DNER. 1996. Programa de investimento em extensão agrária. Documento de Trabalho n. 2/B. DNDR. MAP. Maputo.

————. 1997. *Extension master plan.* October. Maputo: National Directorate of Rural Extension. Maputo: Ministry of Agriculture and Fisheries.

————. 1997a. *Extension master plan,* annex 6. The placement of extension workers within an institutional framework. July. Maputo: DNER, MADER.

————. 1997b. *Extension master plan,* annex. Modalities for housing and means of transportation. August. Maputo: DNER, MADER.

————. 1997c. *Extension master plan,* annex 10. Role of subject matter specialists. Maputo: DNER, MADER.

————. 2001. Manual for outsourcing extension in Mozambique. April. Maputo: DNER, MADER.

————. 2001a. Terms of reference: Outsourcing extension services. April. District of Murrupula, Nampula Province. Maputo: DNER, MADER.

————. 2002. Supervision visit to Gaza province, 27 February to 3 March 2002. Maputo: DNER, MADER.

————. 2002a. The formation and role of extension management committees. Draft. Maputo: DNER, MADER.

————. 2004. *Extension master plan: 2005–2009.* December. Maputo: DNER, MADER.

dos Anjos, F., A. Fumo, Q. Lobo, R.G. Alders, M. P. Young, and B. Bagnol. 2001. Galinhas, gênero e controle de "Newcastle." In *Extensão rural, em Moçambique,* An02. N°4. Maputo: MADER.

Edwards, Michael. 2002. Organizational learning in non-governmental organization: What have we learned? In *The Earthscan reader on NGO management,* edited by Michael Edwards and Alan Fowler. London: Earthscan Publications.

Eicher, Carl K. 1999. *Institutions and the African farmer.* Third Distinguished Economist Lecture. Mexico. D.F: Cimmyt. Reprinted in *Issues in Agriculture* No. 14. September 1999. Washington D.C.: CGIAR Secretariet.

————. 2002. Mozambique: An analysis of the implementation of the extension master plan. Staff Paper No 2002-31. East Lansing, Mich.: Department of Agricultural Economics, Michigan State University. Available at http://agecon.lib.umn.edu/msu/sp02-31.pdf.

————. 2004. Building African models of agricultural extension: A case study of

Mozambique. In *National strategy and reform process. Case studies of international initiatives, Vol. 5.*, edited by Gary Alex and William Rivera. Washington, D.C.: World Bank, USAID, and the Neuchatel Initiative. Available at workshop www.worldbank.org/akis/extension.

Eicher, Carl K., and Mandivamba Rukuni. 2003. The CGIAR in Africa: Past, present and future. OED Working Paper. Washington D.C.: World Bank Operations Evaluation Department. Available at www.worldbank.org/oed/cgiar.

European Commission. 1998. The national program for agricultural development (PROAGRI): The implementation of the programme concept: The way ahead. Maputo: Food Security Unit, European Commission.

———. 1999. Cash cropping in Mozambique: Evolution and prospects. August. Maputo: Food Security Unit, European Commission.

Evenson, Robert E. 1986. The economics of extension. In *Investing in rural extension: Strategies and goals*, edited by Gwyn E. Jones. New York: Elsevier.

———. 2001. Economic impacts of agricultural research and extension. In *Handbook of agricultural economics. vol. 1a: Agricultural production*, edited by Bruce L. Gardner and Gordon C. Rausser, 573–616. New York: Elsevier.

FAO and MADER. 2003. Mozamibque: National program for food security. Plano de Accao de Seguranca Alimentar (2003–8). 28 February. Rome and Maputo: FAO and MADER.

Feder, Gershon, Rinku Murgai, and Jaime B. Quizon. 2004. Sending farmers back to school: The impact of farmer field schools in Indonesia. *Review of Agricultural Economics* 26(1): 45–62.

Friis-Hansen, E., and D. Kisauzi. 2002. Evolution of extension-farmer relationship in Uganda. Paper presented at the workshop *Extension and Rural Development: A Convergence of Views on International Approaches*, 12–15 November 2002. Washington, D.C.: World Bank, USAID and the Neuchatel Initiative.

Garrido-Mirapeix, Julio, and Paolo Toselli. 2002. Agricultural sector programme: From theory to practice. *The Courier* 195 (Nov.–Dec.): 50–51.

Gautam, M., and J. R. Anderson. 1999 *Reconsidering the evidence on the returns to T&V extension in Kenya*. Operations Evaluations Department, Washington D.C.: World Bank.

Gemo, Helder. 2000. Resumo historico da extensão publica em Moçambique. In *Extensão rural em Moçambique*. An01. Nº1, Janeiro. Maputo: MADER.

Gemo, Helder, and William Rivera. 2001. Mozambique's move towards a pluralistic national system of rural extension. Agricultural Research and Extension Network. Network Paper No.10 London: ODI.

———. 2002. Mozambique: Dual public-private services for small farmers. In *contracting for agricultural extension. International case studies and emerging practices*, edited by William M. Rivera and Willem Zijp, 149–54. New York: CABI Publishing.

Goncalves. 1992. Glossário de extensão rural. Maputo: DNDR, Ministério da Agricultura.

Godtland, Erin M., Elisabeth Sadoulet, Alain de Janvery, Rinku Murgai, and Oscar Ortiz. 2004. The impact of farmer field schools on knowledge and productivity: A study of potato farmers in the Peruvian Andes. *Economic Development and Cultural Change* 53(1): 63–92.

Haag, Wayne L. 2000. The SG 2000/DNER partnership experience: Transferring modern science-based crop production technology. *Extensao Rural em Mocambique* 1(3): 39–48.

Halim, Abdul, and Ali Md. Mozahar. 1997. Training and professional development. In *Improving agricultural extension: A reference manual*, edited by Burton Swanson, Robert P Bentz, and Andrew H. Sofranko. Rome: FAO.

Helleiner, Gerald. 1979. AID and dependence in Africa: Issues for recipients. In *The politics of Africa: Dependence and development*, edited by Timothy M. Shaw and Kenneth A. Heard, 221–45. New York: Africana Publishing Co.

Henderson, Sally. 2002. Personal correspondence, e-mail 2 August.

Hilton, Brian, and Ricardo Xavier. 1998-99. Are inputs profitable for smallholder farmers in Northern Zambezia province? Results of fifteen on-farm trials in Gurue district, 1998-99. Maputo: World Vision.

Howard, J, Jose Jaime Jeje, Valerie Kelly, and Duncan Boughton. 2000. Comparing yields and profitability in MARD's high- and low- input maize programs: 1997-98 survey results and analysis. *Flash*, No. 21E. Maputo: MARD Directorate of Economics.

Howard, Julie, Jaquelino Massingue, Jose Jaime Jeje, David Tschirley, Duncan Boughton, and Alexandre Serrano. 2000a. Observations and emerging lessons from the 1998-99 high-input maize program in Nampula province, Mozambique. *Flash*, No 22E. Maputo: MARD Directorate of Economics.

Howard, J., J.J. Jeje, D. Tschirley, P. Strasberg, E. Crawford, and M. Weber. 1998. *What makes agricultural intensification profitable for Mozambican smallholders? An appraisal of the inputs subsector and the 1996-97 DNER/SG 2000 Program.* Research Report no. 31. Maputo: Directorate of Economics, Ministry of Agriculture and Fisheries.

Judd, M.A., J.K. Boyce, and R.E. Evenson. 1986. Investing in agricultural supply. The determinants of agricultural research and extension investment. *Economic Development and Cultural Change* 35(1): 77–113.

Kane, Sam, and Carl K. Eicher. 2004. Foreign aid and the African farmer. Staff Paper 2004-13. East Lansing, Mich.: Department of Agricultural Economics, Michigan State University. August. Available at http://agecon.lib.umn.edu/cgi-bin/pdf_view.pl?paperid=14820&ftype=pdf.

Kanji, N., C. Braga, and W. Mitullah. 2002. Promoção dos direitos relativos à terra em África: Que diferença fazem as ONGs? London: International Institute for Environment and Development (IIED).

Kherallah, Mylene, C. Delgado, E. Gabre-Medhin, N. Minot, and M. Johnson. 2002. *Reforming agricultural markets in Africa.* Baltimore: Johns Hopkins University Press.

Lele, Uma, and Arthur A. Goldsmith. 1989. The development of national agricultural research capacity: India's experience with the Rockefeller Foundation and its significance for Africa. *Economic Development and Cultural Change* 37: 305–43.

Lewis, W. Arthur. 1967. Comment on agricultural taxation in a developing economy. In *Agricultural development and economic growth,* edited by H.R. Southworth and B.F. Johnston, 493–96. Ithaca: Cornell University Press.

Mabota, Anabela, Pedro Arlindo, Antonio Paulo, and Cynthia Donovan. 2003. Market information: A low cost tool for agricultural market development? *Flash.* No. 37E. MADER Directorate of Economics.

Macedo, Jamil et al. 2003. *Brazil country paper for the CGIAR meta-evaluation* (OED). Working Paper. Washington, D.C.: World Bank Operations Evaluation Department.

Malone, V.M. 1984. In-service training and staff development. In *Agricultural extension: A reference manual,* edited by Burton Swanson, Robert P. Benz and Andrew H. Sofranko. Rome: FAO.

Manor, James. 1998. *The political economy of democratic decentralization*. Washington, D.C.: World Bank.

Matsumoto, Tetsuo, Donald Plucknett, and Kunio Takase. 2003. *Evaluation of the Sasakawa global 2000 program in Mozambique, 1995–2002*. Tokyo: Sasakawa Africa Association.

Mavale, A.P. 1995. Epidemiology and control of Newcastle disease in rural poultry in Mozambique. Masters Degree Thesis. Veterinary Epidiomology and Economics Research Unit. The Department of Agriculture, The University of Reading.

Mellor, John. 1976. *The new economics of growth: A strategy for India and the developing world*. Ithaca: Cornell University Press.

Messiter, Bill. 1999. Comparison of cash crop returns to the family sector in Manica. February. Maputo: Africare-Mozamibique.

Morss, E. 1984. Institutional destruction resulting from donor and project proliferation in sub-Saharan African countries. *World Development* 12(4): 465–70.

Mucavele, C. E. 2000. The economics of smallholder rice producers in Bilene-Macia district, Southern Mozambique. Faculty of Biological and Agricultural Sciences. University of Pretoria.

Mucavele, Custodio. 2002. Public extension services. June. Maputo: DNER.

Nahdy, Silim, Francis Byekwaso, and David Nielson. 2002. Decentralized farmer-owned extension in Uganda. In *Food security in a changing Africa*, edited by Steven Breth, 38–50. Geneva: Centre for Applied Studies in International Negotiations.

Ndulu, Benno J. 2004. Human capital flight: Stratification, globalization and challenges to tertiary higher education in Africa. *Journal of Higher Education in Africa* 2(1): 57–91.

New Partnership for Africa's Development (NEPAD). 2002. *Comprehensive Africa agricultural development program*. Pretoria: NEPAD Secretariat.

Nhancale, I.T. 2000. Enhancing the maize productivity of small-scale farmers through zero tillage practices in Manica province, Mozambique. Cape Coast, Ghana: School of Agriculture. University of Cape Coast.

Nielson, David. 2002. Discussion: Challenges to extension service delivery. In *Food security in a changing Africa*, edited by Steven A. Breth, 61–62. Geneva: Centre for Applied Studies in International Negotiations.

Nielson, David, and Peter Bazeley. 2000. The search for impact and whether "outreach" is the answer. Nairobi: Kenya Agricultural Research Institute.

Pavignani, E., and V. Hauck. 2002. Pooling of technical assistance in Mozamibque: Innovative practices and challenges. ECDPM Discussion Paper 39.. Maastricht: ECDPM.

Phillips, Ron, and Alex Serrano. 1999. Developing self-managed outgrower capacity in Zambia and Mozambique. March. Nampula: CLUSA.

Population Council. 1978. *A chronicle of the first twenty-five years, 1952–1977.* New York: Praeger.

PROAGRI. 1998. PRO-AGRI: *National program of agrarian development:* 1998 to 2003. Vol. I—executive summary. Vol. II—master document. Vol. III—annexes. Maputo: Ministry of Agriculture and Fisheries.

———. 2000. *Mozambique PROAGI: Institutional reform of the agricultural research system.* Maputo: MADER.

———. 2001. PROAGRI joint review meeting: Aide memoire 25 May. Maputo: MADER.

———. 2001a. PROAGRI Mozambique: Annual financial management meeting, aide memoire, 21 November. Maputo: MADER.

———. 2002. PROAGRI Mozambique: Annual review. May 2002. Aide memoire. Maputo: MADER.

———. 2002a. Mozambique: Annual Financial Management Meeting, 25–27 November. Aide Memoire. Maputo: MADER.

———. 2002b. Evaluation. Main report. Volume 1. Maputo: MADER.

PROAGRI II. 2004. *PROAGRI II: Strategy document.* March. Maputo: MADER.

Quizon, Jaime, Gershon Feder, and Rinku Murgai. 2001. Fiscal sustainability of agricultural extension: The case of the farmer field school approach. *Journal of International Agricultural and Extension Education* 8(1): 13–23.

Rice, E. B. 1971. *Extension in the Andes.* Washington, D.C.: USAID.

Rivera, William M., and John W. Carey. 1997. Privatizing agricultural extension. In *Improving agricultural extension: A reference manual,* edited by Burton E. Swanson, Robert P. Bentz, and Andrew J. Sofranko, 203–11. Rome: FAO.

Rivera, William M., and William Zijp, editors. 2002. *Contracting for agricultural extension: International case studies and emerging practices.* New York: CABI Publishing.

Rivera, William M., and Gary Alex. 2004. The continuing role of government in pluralistic extension systems. *Journal of International Agricultural and Extension Education* 11(3): 41–52.

Rola, A. C., J. B. Quizon, and S. B. Jamias. 2002. Do farmer field school graduates retain and share what they learn?: An investigation in Iloilo, Phillippines. *Journal of International Agricultural and Extension Education* 5(1): 65–75.

Roling, Niels, and Jules N. Pretty. 1997. Extension's role in sustainable agricultural development. In *Improving agricultural extension: A reference manual*, edited by Burton E. Swanson, Robert P. Benz, and Andrew F. Sofranko, 181–91. Rome: FAO.

Royal Tropical Institute. 2002. Mozambique PROAGRI: Institutional reform of the agricultural research system. December. Amsterdam: Royal Tropical Institute.

Rukuni, Mandivamba. 1996. *A framework for crafting demand-driven national agricultural research institutions in southern Africa*. Staff Paper No. 96. East Lansing, Michigan. Department of Agricultural Economics. Michigan State University.

Rukuni, M., M. J. Blackie, and C. K. Eicher. 1998. Crafting smallholder-driven agricultural research systems in Southern Africa. *World Development* 26(6): 1073–87.

Ruotsi, J. 2003. *Agricultural marketing companies as sources of smallholder credit: Experiences, insights and potential donor role*. Rome: International Fund for Agricultural Development.

Rusike J., D. Masendeke, S. J. Twomlow, and G. M.Heinrich. 2004. Impact of farmer field schools on adoption of soil water and nutrient management technologies in dry areas of Zimbabwe. Report no. 12. Bulawayo, Zimbabwe: ICRISAT.

Sasakawa Africa Association. 2002. Mozambique: Sasakawa Africa Newsletter. April.

———. 2005. *Feeding the future*. Newsletter of the Sasakawa African Association. March.

Sousa, Daniel. 2002. BTOR: PROAGRI-joint supervision visit to Sofala province. Agricultural Services Group, 1–9 August 2002. Maputo: World Bank.

South Africa. 2001. *The strategic plan for South African agriculture*. Pretoria: Department of Agriculture

Sulemane Jose A., and Steve Kayizzi-Mugerwa. 2003. The Mozambican civil service: Incentives, reforms and performance. In *Reforming Africa's institutions: Ownership, incentives and capabilities*, edited by Steve Kayizzi-Mugerwa,

199–226. New York: United Nations Press.

Swanson, Burton E. 2004. Extension strategies for poverty alleviation in a global economy. Paper Presented at the 2d International Conference on Agricultural Education on and Environment. Suwon, Republic of Korea, 14 October.

Swanson, Burton E., and Mohamed M. Samy. 2002. Developing an extension partnership among public, private, and nongovernmental organizations. *Journal of International Agricultural and Extension Education* 9(1): 5–10.

Tawonezvi, Patrick. 2003. Personal correspondence. e-mail, 16 April.

Tschirley, David L., and Rui Benfica. 2001. Smallholder agriculture, wage labor and rural poverty alleviation in land-abundant areas of Africa: Evidence from Mozambique. *The Journal of Modern African Studies* 39(2): 333–58.

Van den Ban, A. W., and H. S. Hawkins. 1996. *Agricultural extension.* 2d ed. Oxford: Blackwell.

Walker, Tom. 1981. A package versus a gradient approach in the development and delivery of technology in dry land agriculture. Andra Pradesh, India: ICRISAT.

Weatherspoon, Dave D., and Thomas Reardon. 2003. The rise of supermarkets in Africa: Implications for agrifood systems and the rural poor. *Development Policy Review* 21(3): 1–17.

Wentling, Mark. 2002. Personal correspondence, e-mail. July 29.

White, Robert, and Carl K. Eicher. 1999. *NGOs and the African farmer: A skeptical perspective.* Staff paper No. 99–1. East Lansing, Michigan: Department of Agricultural Economics, Michigan State University. Available at http://agecon.lib.umn.edu/msu.html.

World Bank. 1985. *Agricultural research and extension: An evaluation of the World Bank's Experience.* Washington, D.C.: World Bank.

———. 1999. Agricultural sector public expenditure program (PROAGRI). Project Appraisal Document, 22 January. Report 18862 Moz.. Washington D.C.: World Bank.

———. 2000. Mozambique: Growth performance and reform agenda. Report no 20601-MZ. Washington, D.C.: World Bank.

———. 2001. Agricultural services and rehabilitation project, Mozambique. Implementation Completion Report, 12 July. Washington, D.C.: World Bank.

———. 2002. News Release No 2002/273/S, 10 April. Washington, D.C.: World Bank.

————. 2002a. *From action to impact: The Africa region's rural strategy.* Washington, D.C.: World Bank.

————. 2003. Final report on the workshop on extension and rural development, November 12–15, World Bank, Washington D.C. World Bank. Available at

————. 2003a. A multi-country agricultural productivity program (MAPP) for Africa. January. Draft. Washington, D.C.: World Bank.

————. 2003b. *Reaching the rural poor: A renewed strategy for rural development.* Washington D.C.: World Bank.

————. 2004. *Agricultural investment sourcebook.* Washington, D.C.: Agriculture and rural development. World Bank.

Ye, Sergio, R. J. Ndoro, C. Mucavele, J. Nduna, and S. Tsimba. 2003. Avaliacao preliminar do impacto do sistema unificado de extensao e do sistema nacional de extensao. Lichinga. Niassa. May.